the complete book of

soft dolls

By the same author:
Creative Soft Toy Making, 1974
How to make Dinosaurs and Dragons, 1976

the complete book of

soft dolls

Pamela Peake

Line drawings by the author

DAVID & CHARLES
Newton Abbot   London   North Pomfret (Vt)

British Library Cataloguing in Publication Data

Peake, Pamela
    The complete book of soft dolls.
    1. Dollmaking   2. Soft toy making
    I. Title
    745.59'22   TT175

ISBN 0-7153-7595-4

Designs, text and line illustrations © Pamela Peake, 1979

First published 1979
Second impression 1980
Third impression 1982
Fourth impression 1987

Printed in Great Britain by
Butler & Tanner Ltd, Frome and London
for David & Charles Publishers plc
Brunel House Newton Abbot Devon

Published in the United States of America
by David & Charles Inc
North Pomfret Vermont 05053 USA

Contents

To John
and Susan
and Katherine

1 Soft dolls
- a brief history

Some of the earliest three-dimensional representations of the human form come from graves and there is considerable debate whether these functioned as dolls or had some deeper religious significance as idols. Children have a natural ability to see toys in all manner of objects and it is quite feasible that a doll, no matter how crudely fashioned, was one of the earliest playthings. These dolls could have been improvised from material close at hand such as sticks and stones. Consequently many would have had a short life of no more than a few hours or days, and therefore are rarely preserved in the archaeological record.

So human images have, at least, a dual purpose and we have gradually attached different levels of appreciation to these. In more highly developed societies concepts of beauty have reached extremely sophisticated levels. For example, in Africa there were the Benin bronzes, in Japan, the Festival dolls, while in Europe, there were the Automata and fashion dolls. In all of these, we see the skill and pride of the craftsman.

The development of dolls reaches its highest level in Japan and here there is no clear distinction between simple playthings and beautifully costumed ornaments. Indeed there is a single word — ningyo — to describe all small human images. For at least 1,000 years display dolls were used in festivals for ancestor worship, purification and symbolism. Their function gradually evolved and they are now used to instruct Japanese children in social customs and duty. Doll play was also developed during this time, culminating in the bunraku puppets which must surely be the closest man can get to making a working image of himself.

The development of soft dolls is usually associated with the production of cloth and consequently the techniques of spinning and weaving; there were alternative methods of producing a similar effect such as crocheting or using felt and animal skins, but the nature of these materials has meant that very few soft dolls have survived. The earliest examples show that the Egyptians, Romans and Peruvians fashioned dolls from strips of rag bound together, or by cutting, stitching and stuffing pieces of material. It is usually presumed that these dolls were play objects and served a similar function to those produced today. Indeed the design of soft dolls shows remarkably few innovations since these early examples. Function, design and the nature of the material appear to have been inseparably linked, as children will always need a soft, cuddly toy.

The Industrial Revolution of the nineteenth century saw the invention of the sewing machine and therefore for many people the end of long, tedious hand sewing. Cottons were cheap and consequently there was a boom in home dressmaking. This burst of enthusiasm passed to doll-making with the result that the last hundred years has seen more change and improvement in soft dolls than ever before. This change was undoubtedly encouraged by the simultaneous development of hard dolls. The public demanded more realism and as a result manufacturers developed dolls that could open and shut eyes, turn heads, move limbs, and eventually very sophisticated dolls that cried, talked, walked, fed and could even swim. Apart from technique, however, the biggest change was in design with the advent of the baby doll. Prior to this time, all dolls were fashioned as adults, even if they were dressed as babies. The popularity of the baby doll still continues today while adult dolls are usually only made by craftswomen. The latter are certainly not play dolls, rather an art form that appears as a sculptured personal comment.

From the beginning of the twentieth century, educationalists, psychologists and artists have analysed our image of the doll. They have spurned the very sophisticated dolls of the previous century, insisting that they gave the child no chance to use its imagination. What was needed was a simple baby or child-like doll that the child could identify with. It had to be realistic in appearance but devoid of any gimmicks. Safety, washability and softness were of paramount importance. So the cloth doll was top of the list, for it offered emotional security and, through play, an awareness of the world around. The concept of the soft doll as a beautiful baby or toddler was developed and explored on both sides of the Atlantic by a wide range of artists and designers. Such individuals as Kathe Krüse, Grace Putnam, Martha Chase and Elena Konig di Scavini were outstanding.

There have always been people who wished to express their creative feelings even through something which was functional. They needed the sense of personal satisfaction and enjoyment. Doll-makers are no exception, for the ability to create dolls straight from the subconscious is not linked to some form of formal training or knowledge of techniques. The only requisite is the desire. This book will help you with some of the first steps and then you are launched. Let the colour photographs and illustrations guide you towards your own interpretation. Then enjoy yourself.

Finally, a cautionary note; when creating your doll always remember its final use, whether it is to be for play or display. In this book you will find designs for a wide range of soft dolls, some of which are quite unsuitable for small children. So be selective, be safety conscious.

2 Doll anatomy

When we were young we must all have drawn simple stick figures, for this was the easiest way to depict our families and friends. Soon clothes would have been added and the proportions changed to make adults and children. Faces became increasingly important and were often drawn correspondingly larger so that the stick figure people could be shown as smiling or crying. Figure 1 shows a selection of stick figures.

Fig 1   The human figure as seen by different age groups

As adults, we tend to approach drawing simple graphic people in two very different ways. There are the drawings that are reminiscent of fashion illustrations. Here the greatest emphasis is placed on long, flowing bodies and limbs hinting at idealized elegance. Heads, on the other hand, are very small and faces so simple that they frequently lack all features and hence are devoid of expression. Just think of some of the boutique window models. They are pure sophistication of limbs!

The second type of drawing concentrates on the head by exaggerating the features, while the body and limbs are of very secondary importance. This is the type of drawing favoured by comic artists and doodlers, where the face says it all.

The development of your dolls as you design them will follow a similar pattern. Some will resemble stick figures with large heads that have simply been fleshed out while boudoir dolls are fabric interpretations of the long legged fashion drawings. Needle sculpture is a technique that will enable you to develop exaggerated features. No matter what style of doll you make, whether young or old, tall or short, fat or slim, it will be constructed according to well-recognized laws of proportion.

Body proportions

In this instance, 'proportions' means the relationship of parts to one another and the conventional unit of measurement that is used for dolls as well as for people is the head. This is an established practice amongst artists, where the total height of an adult is taken as being seven and a half to eight times the length of the head. Figure 2 shows how these proportions change with age. Young children have relatively larger heads and shorter limbs. For instance a youngster of five years has a total height of five heads which is an easy proportion to remember. Most rag dolls are designed as children, having proportions suggestive of an eight-year-old — that is, total height equals six times the length of the head.

In Figure 2 the arms are drawn hanging down beside the body at rest, and in every instance, no matter what the age, they reach halfway down the thigh and the thumbs face forwards. When the arms are raised the thumbs can either point downwards or upwards. The former is an antisocial gesture while the latter, which shows the palms, is more desirable as it is a welcoming, friendly gesture. The arms, including the hands, are generally as long as the legs. However whereas an adult can reach his arm over his head and touch his ear, a young child cannot. Another relationship that is worth noting is that the hand, with fingers outstretched, is large enough to cover the face.

There are always variations to rules and body proportions are no exception. Old people, when viewed from the side, have a different posture from younger people. Necks are often lost and chins jut out quite forcibly. At the other end of the age scale, infants have different proportions again and several anatomical features that need to be incorporated into their patterns. A young baby of a few months old has a long body with a short, thin neck supporting a large head. The legs are bent at the knees and pulled up towards the body. They are of even thickness down their length with small, almost insignificant feet. The arms are also bent and the hands tend to be kept clenched as a fist.

Your own observation of people should provide all the information you need to capture the essential features necessary to incorporate in your design for a particular character.

10

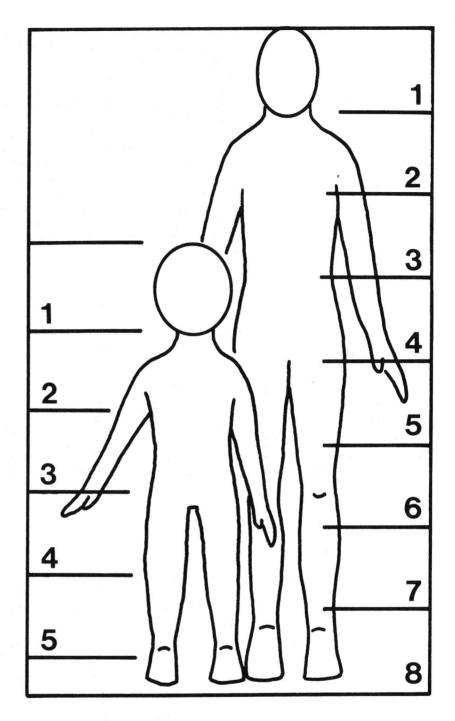

Fig 2   Body proportions of a five-year-old and an adult

Position of facial features

Positioning the features correctly on a face frequently provides more problems than any other aspect of doll-making. Whereas the body and clothes can be put together in a way that would be acceptable even if the standard left something to be desired, the whole character of the doll depends on the presentation of the facial features. Although the features may be very simple, slight variations can make all the difference between the doll being accepted or rejected. Consequently the development of the face becomes the most important aspect of doll-making. There are fundamental guide-lines that

11

determine the position of eyes, nose and mouth and thereby remove the need for any guesswork. Furthermore the position of the features on the face indicates whether the doll represents a child or an adult, while the features themselves determine whether it is a male or female doll.

The best way to understand faces is to make diagrams of your own. Start by drawing an egg-shaped outline for an adult head as shown in Figure 3. Although there will be variations in the proportions of different faces, such differences can be readily accommodated within the overall scheme. Now divide the head in half vertically by ruling a line from A to A then horizontally by ruling another line from B to B. The lower half of the head is the face area and this must be divided horizontally into quarters by ruling lines C to C, D to D and E to E. By starting with an adult head you will be able to check off the position of the features on the diagram by observing your own face in a mirror.

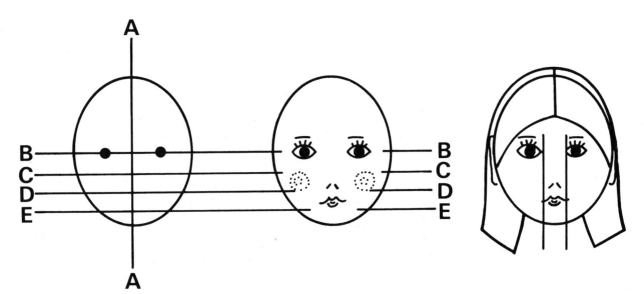

Fig 3   Facial features of an adult

The eyes lie on the line B which is halfway down the head. The nostrils lie on the line D which is halfway between the eyes and the chin while the line E passes just beneath the lower lip for a female or through the lower lip for a male. The remaining guide-line for faces

Fig 4   Facial features of a child

is determined by the width of the eyes and their position on line B. You will see from Figure 3 that the eyes are spaced apart by their own width and that the nose and mouth tend to lie within the same spacing.

12

Finally, run your finger in a line across your face from your nostrils towards the side of your head and you should feel the bottom edge of your ear. The top of the ears are level with your eyebrows and again you should run your fingers across your face to feel the relationship. Figure 3 shows the position of the features mentioned with the eyebrows above line B. The cheeks lie between lines C and D.

The head of a child is generally characterized by a more rounded shape and a high forehead. Figure 4 shows how the head is again subdivided in exactly the same way as the adult's head. However, the eyes and ears are positioned lower down on the face while the eyebrows just touch line B. The eyes are also slightly further apart. The position of the nose and mouth remain unaltered.

Practise positioning the features by drawing several diagrams until you can do it confidently without having to rule all the guidelines.

3 Heads, faces and hair

Many of the important character-making features of soft dolls are found on the head, for the face and hairstyle quickly indicate age and sex and if the individual is happy or sad. Furthermore the construction of the head determines whether the doll has a realistic sculptured face or a flat face with embroidered, painted or appliquéd features. The heads of traditional rag dolls are invariably flat or two-dimensional with only the eyes and mouth represented. Consequently the range of emotions which can be portrayed are limited and generally gentle. In contrast a much wider range of facial features, and therefore characters, can be developed from a three-dimensional sculptured head. The inclusion of noses and chins enables quite positive and forceful characters to be depicted as well as the more delicate.

In Table 1, the dolls of the book are listed together with their hairstyles and the various methods of constructing heads, necks and faces. Reference should be made to the instructions for the relevant doll, where detailed information is provided.

Heads

Basically the head consists of an oval or egg shape that sits on a well-formed cylinder which is the neck. Although there are many ways of making such a shape the method chosen will depend on the type of doll being made, the ingenuity of the maker and last, but not least, the needs of the recipient.

1. Simple ball heads: a perfectly adequate head can be obtained by gathering up a circle of fabric and enclosing a knob of stuffing before closing off. The gathers can easily be hidden at the back of the head. A tube of stockinette tied off on either side of a ball of stuffing is a variation.

2. Outline heads: in its simplest form this includes flat two-dimensional dolls where the body outline and that of the head are continuous. There is often no additional shaping. Although the face is usually shown on the flat surface looking forwards it is also possible to make it facing sideways with the outline of the head following the profile of the chin, mouth, nose and forehead.

3. Shaped heads: this is a very diverse group for it includes all those heads where a three-dimensional shape is achieved by the addition of darts and gussets or the repetition of many segments. Humpty Dumpty, for example, is made from four similar segments which have been divided so that there is an upper and lower half depicting respectively the head and the body. In this book darts are used to give breadth to the top of the head while gussets are usually placed centrally so that shape can be added to the cheeks and forehead.

4. Soft-sculptured heads: there are two different ways of making this type of head; one consists of adding to and building up the form while the other removes unwanted bulk by the use of judiciously placed stitches rather than a knife or chisel. Annette provides an example of the former and Joe of the latter (see Plates 5 and 8). Both methods are exciting and dynamic, for the head, and in particular the

14

Table 1   Head construction:
The heads, faces and hairstyles illustrated in this book

Doll	Head	Neck	Face	Hairstyle
Elizabeth, Erika	outline	continuous	embroidered	embroidered curls
Emily, Lavender Lil	outline	continuous	pen	skein wig
Katrina	outline	continuous	appliquéd felt	skein wig long hair
Girls and Boys	outline	continuous	embroidered	embroidered skein wigs plaits
Butcher, Baker Candlestick-maker	outline	continuous	painted	painted curls
Hilary, Hinemoa Harry	outline	continuous	embroidered	skein wig short hair and curls
Bubbles	outline	continuous	appliquéd felt and embroidered	curls
Rodriguez Rodney	stockinette tube	body extension	button eyes moustache	bundles
Arabella	shaped	body extension	appliquéd felt and embroidered	ponytail
Mandy	shaped	body extension	embroidered	skein wig with fringe
Victoria	shaped	end to end	embroidered	skein wig and ponytail
Cheko	shaped	head extension	appliquéd felt	curls
Norman	shaped	end to end disc jointed	embroidered	skein wig short hair
Annette	soft sculptured	head extension swivel joint	colour pencils	skein wig bun
Gerry	shaped	continuous	colour pencils	bundles
Sleepy Sue Wee Willie Winkie	shaped	head extension	appliquéd felt and embroidered	skein wig and fringe
Wendy	shaped	body extension	embroidered	skein wig plaits
Jane	soft sculptured	body extension	needle modelled	skein wig
Julia	face mask	body extension	colour pencils	skein wig

Doll	Head	Neck	Face	Hairstyle
Lucy, Tony	face mask	continuous	coloured pencils	none
Twins	stockinette tube	continuous	embroidered	none
Suffolk Maid	simple ball	none	pen	mohair
Humpty Dumpty	shaped	continuous	appliquéd felt	bundles
Rebecca	soft sculptured	head extension	button eyes	skein wig long with beads
Ruth	simple ball	head extension	bead eyes	skein wig ponytail
Caroline	shaped	none	embroidered	skein wig ringlets
Louisa	shaped	body extension	embroidered	ringlets earphones plaited bun
Joe	soft sculptured	continuous	colour pencils	bundles

face, grows under your touch. Each head will be unique and unrepeatable.

The building method consists of adding layers of padding to a head-former. The chin, cheeks and forehead are all developed to the required degree by the addition of extra padding. The nose is often formed by a large bead. The entire head is then covered by a skin of stretch fabric, such as stockinette, which is glued in place. This outer skin has a softening effect on the underlying features. The second, or needle-modelled method, involves the placement of many fine stitches in a skin of stretch fabric that encloses a ball of stuffing. The form of the nose, chin and mouth is made by careful adjustment of the tension on the stitches thereby changing the position of the stuffing. Likewise eye sockets can be sunk into the head by pulling stitches right through the ball of stuffing.

5. Face masks: this illustrates the progression towards a controlled form of sculpture as the face is made on a mould and is therefore repeatable. The technique is illustrated by Julia and Lucy (see Plates 6 and 7). Very sophisticated expressions and features can be incorporated and the method has been used most effectively in the construction of historical costume models. You can make the mould from either clay or plasticine, but it is also possible to use the face of a commercially produced doll. If a hollow plastic head or face is used, it would be wise to reinforce it by filling the back or centre with either candle-wax or some form of plaster. It can also be embedded in a ball of plasticine which has the advantage of providing a steady base.

The mould is greased with Vaseline to prevent the mask sticking to it. Two squares of muslin and another of either stockinette or felt, are cut large enough to completely cover the face. These are then soaked in paste, wallpaper paste being eminently suitable. Squeeze the pieces of fabric to remove any excess paste and lay them over the mould on the diagonal. The pieces of muslin are positioned first, one on top of the other, followed by the stockinette or felt. Press each layer of fabric down on to the mould, working into all the details of the face with a fine stick. Remove any excess paste. The mask should be left to dry slowly on the mould for a few days. While it is still wet and springy, the fabric should be pressed back down firmly on to the mould from time to time.

When dry, remove the mask carefully from the mould and trim the edges to a suitable shape for attaching to a head-former.

Faces

It is unnecessary to work all the facial features in detail, for simplicity is the keynote to success. Indeed the addition of eyes alone will often provide a wealth of expression, sufficient to give your doll an individual and appealing character. The inclusion of too much information or detail can lead to confusion and destroy the expression which you are trying to create.

The various techniques used to make the faces in this book are all listed in Table 1, pages 15-16. Follow the guide-lines outlined in the previous chapter and the ideas shown in Figure 5 for positioning and working the features.

Fig 5 Suggestions for facial features.
Top row embroidered eyebrows and felt shapes.
Second row embroidered eyes, padded nose and embroidered nose.
Third row felt eyes with embroidered eyelashes, sleeping eyes, padded nose suitable for a clown and embroidered nostrils.
Fourth row felt cheeks with cross stitch and buttonhole stitch and embroidered cheeks.
Bottom row a selection of felt shapes and embroidered mouths

The faces have been embroidered, stitched or coloured directly on to the finished dolls after the heads have been stuffed, for this is the only way to ensure that you position the face in the right place. The painted flat dolls in Chapter 6 are the exception to this rule. This is because the paint has to be made colour-fast by ironing, and this can only be done before the dolls are constructed.

A soft pencil is used to lightly draw the facial features directly on to the doll and any unwanted pencil marks can be removed with a white plastic rubber. Test the pencil and rubber on a scrap of fabric first, before marking the doll.

Start by finding the hair-line then mark in the eyes, followed by two small dots for the nostrils and lastly the mouth. If you feel hesitant about drawing freehand, pin a piece of tracing paper over the face and draw the features on this. Remove the tracing paper and fold it in half to check that both sides of the drawing are identical. If not, then select the best side and trace off the other half. Place the tracing against the doll and press off the features from the reverse side. The pencilled face is now ready to be either coloured with fibre-tip pens, dampened pencils or embroidered with three strands of embroidery thread.

There is no need to draw a face on a doll that is having felt features. Simply cut out the pieces of felt neatly and move them around on the face until you find a pleasing arrangement. Hem the felt in place with small stitches in preference to gluing.

Hair

There are many different yarns and fabrics that can be successfully used for representing hair. They include the obvious like wool yarn of all thicknesses, stranded embroidery thread, soft cotton, dishcloth cotton, fur fabric, felt and artificial hair. Less obvious, but still worth considering, are plumber's tow, hessian, string, mohair, angora, astrakhan, poodle cloth, raffia, leather thongs, lurex threads, tape, ribbon and fabric strips. These materials can either be applied directly to the head and styled in position or first made into wigs and skull caps which are then attached to the doll. Small dolls generally have embroidered hair while larger dolls have a variety of wool-yarn hairstyles that are usually made from one of three basic methods:

1. Skein wigs: this is the most popular method for making hair because it can be styled in so many different ways (see Fig 6). It is equally suitable for both young and old characters, as well as for male and female hairstyles.

Determine the amount of wool needed by measuring from the centre parting to the desired length. Double this length and add 7.5cm (3in) to counteract both the tension from winding and the difference in height of head from forehead to crown. Now wind the wool into a skein or hank of the required length, cut the loops at either end and sew a central parting to hold the skein together. Position wig on the head and back stitch through the parting to the doll beneath. If necessary, the wig can be held in place with glue.

A variation of this basic method is the addition of a fringe. Wind a second skein and sew a parting a few inches back from one end, the distance being determined by the length of the fringe required. Figure 6 shows how the two skeins are placed on the head. The long portion of this second skein is used for adding more hair to the back of the head.

Fig 6 Variety of hairstyles obtained from a skein wig. Ringlets are made by twisting together several long strands of wool; then, without releasing the tension, place a finger in the middle of the twisted strands and fold the end up to the head. Hold the ends firmly and remove finger from middle so that the twists coil on themselves to form a ringlet

18

2. Ponytails, chignon and pompadour: these styles require very long hair that is generally pulled back from the hair-line around the face and nape of neck. Measure the length of hair required, double it then cut all the wool to this length. Sew the wool together along a central line arranging the wool so that the length of this line is sufficient to encircle the head. The wig is attached to the head by sewing along this same line of stitching which in turn becomes the hair-line of the doll (see Fig 7). Pull all the wool back towards the crown of the head and arrange in the style required.

Fig 7   Ponytail, chignon and pompadour hairstyles

Fig 8   *Left* short curls made by winding wool around a Quadframe (*above*) or a cardboard template (*below*) and then sewing through the centre. *Right* several lengths of these curls are then arranged spirally on the head

3. Short curls: this hairstyle is made from long streamers of curls that are usually prepared by winding wool around narrow strips of stiff paper, sewing along the centre and then tearing away the paper

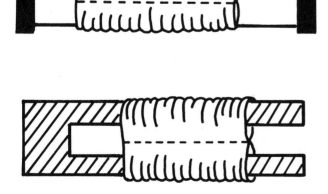

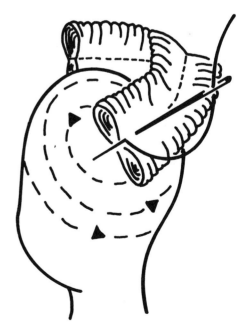

on either side of the stitching. This is a tedious process that can be speeded up considerably by using a template such as a Quadframe, hairpin crochet fork, hardboard fringe-maker or a proprietary rug fork that is sold with some sewing machines (see Fig 8). The streamers of curls are sewn to the head spirally from the centre of the crown outwards. The length of streamers that you will need depends on the depth of the curls and how close you sew the different rows together.

4 Bodies, arms and legs

The central body or trunk acts as a foundation for the attachment of the head and limbs. It is frequently little more than a simple bag of stuffing that will be covered by clothes. More attention has always been placed on shaping the limbs and developing the articulation at the shoulders and hips. Hinges and joints allow the dolls to sit or stand and limbs to move independently, thereby greatly increasing the play value of the dolls and their desirability. The ultimate development of this trend towards complete animation is exhibited by string puppets which are, in effect, fully articulated dolls.

Bodies

Cloth bodies have been made throughout the ages as the material could be readily obtained and easily hand sewn. Moreover, the design of the bodies has always been rather conservative, as there has never been any reason to alter the basic shape. For a very long time dolls have tended to be flat-chested and sexless, gender being indicated by face, hair and clothes.

In the nineteenth century, commercially produced dolls with bisque, china or composition heads frequently had cloth and kid bodies. These dolls were invariably dressed as adults. However during the early part of the twentieth century the fashion changed and there was a preference for bisque-headed baby dolls that had simple muslin or stockinette bodies. The advent of plastics produced a major revolution in the production of commercial dolls and now the entire dolls are moulded in these substances. The modern trend still favours baby dolls, but teenage fashion dolls have appeared and proved very popular with their shapely waists and small busts.

The range of bodies exhibited by the dolls in this book relates more to function than to fashion. The majority have a simple, basic body shape which is the same both front and back. Shoulders have been developed as a broad platform for the attachment of the arms, whether the latter are hinged or articulated. Costume dolls need more shapely bodies to show off the clothes and this is achieved by the insertion of appropriately positioned darts.

Some of the dolls have been designed to sit and support themselves. This involves adding a functional hip hinge or joint and shaping the bottom either in the pattern cutting or by incorporating gathers, darts, gussets or folds. Arabella, Wendy, Norman, Annette, Gerry, Miss Victoria and Mandy are dolls that illustrate these features.

Although waists are sometimes shaped, the possibility of making a doll bend in this region is largely ignored. The pattern for Cheko the Clown includes a swing-hinged waist that is similar to the conventional articulation found in soft-bodied string puppets. Consequently he is able to exhibit a wide range of flexibility and holds a unique position amongst the dolls in this book. Cheko is truly a performing doll.

Arms and legs

The majority of rag dolls have simple tubes for arms and legs that

Fig 9   Development of arm shapes

taper towards the hands and feet. Occasionally more shaping is required but even so it can never be as realistic as that found in manufactured hard dolls. A satisfactory balance between simplicity and realism is achieved by gently curving the top half of the upper and lower portion of each limb as in Figure 9. This will effectively thicken the limbs in the muscle areas. The arms will also appear more graceful and relaxed if they are bent slightly at the elbow. However the shape of the limbs will ultimately be determined by the method of articulation and influenced to a lesser extent by the style of clothes and age depicted by the doll.

Feet

Frequently the feet are formed by no more than a bend at the bottom of the leg with additional shaping sometimes being provided by a sole or darts. Socks and shoes then hide all the shortcomings such as lack of toes. If a doll is to stand unaided it must be designed so that the centre of gravity lies directly above the feet. Only then will the doll balance. Stability can be increased either by adding weights to the toes or by enlarging the relative size of the feet and shoes.

Hands

Hands are one of the most expressive parts of the human body as their gestures can so quickly and easily indicate a whole range of feelings and character. Many of these expressions can be usefully incorporated in the dolls although it is better not to try for too much definition in small dolls and likewise knockabout rag dolls. In both these instances it is sufficient to have a simple outline shape with a separate thumb.

Larger dolls with outline hand shapes usually have the fingers indicated by rows of top stitching. It is very rare to see cloth dolls with separate fingers, possibly because of the skill needed to stitch

22

and turn such tiny parts. However, leather and felt can be used to make separate fingers as both these materials are non-fraying and can therefore be stitched on the surface. Kid-bodied dolls had separate fingers stitched around a wire frame but they looked more like gloves than hands. Scavini made her felt dolls, the Lenci dolls, with second and third fingers stitched together and all the others separate — a feature that became one of her trademarks. Because hands are so expressive they tend to be exaggerated in puppetry. The size is increased while the cluttered effect is overcome by the convention of having thumb and three fingers only, as in Cheko the Clown.

The articulation of limbs

The very nature of fabric imposes certain limitations on developing sophisticated joints. Nevertheless doll-makers have plagiarized ideas from hard dolls and have experimented with different techniques using thread, wire, elastic, discs and buttons to develop ingenious methods of articulation. More techniques were developed during the nineteenth century than at any other time, when all manner of joints and complex darts and gussets were devised in an effort to articulate the kid bodies attached to the commercially produced porcelain heads.

Table 2 Limb articulation:
The hinges and joints illustrated in this book

Doll	Shoulders	Hips
Bubbles Hilary Hinemoa Harry Humpty Dumpty	swing hinge	swing hinge
Rodriguez Rodney	lap hinge	swing hinge
Arabella Wendy	swing hinge and swing hinge elbows	swing hinge and swing hinge knees
Victoria	socket hinge	swing hinge and swing hinge knees
Mandy	lap hinge	parcel hinge
Cheko	lap hinge and gusset elbows	swing hinge and gusset knees
Annette	disc joint	disc joint
Norman Gerry	pivot joint	pivot joint
Louisa	elastic elbow	swing hinge and swing hinge knees
Suffolk Maid Jane Julia	pipe cleaner elbows	- - -

The dolls of Chapters 7, 8 and 9 display a wide range of different hinges and joints, many of which have been used successfully for hundreds of years. They are all listed in Table 2 and some of them are illustrated in Figure 10 and Plate 1; instructions for making these joints and hinges are given with the relevant doll.

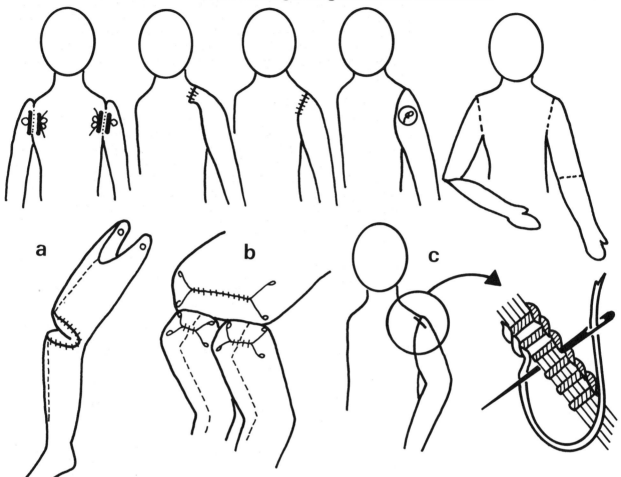

Fig 10   Limb articulation.
Top row different shoulder joints, *left to right* disc, lap hinge, socket, pivot and stitch-hinged arm with stitch-hinged elbow.
Bottom row (a) a gusset-hinge knee and a *'ne plus ultra'* hip joint; (b) parcel hinge for hips; (c) a double buttonhole bar for a shoulder joint

5 Making the dolls

This chapter contains all the basic information needed to make the fabric dolls illustrated in this book. It should be read carefully before proceeding further so that you are familiar with the more general aspects of pattern-making and doll construction. You will then be able to concentrate on the special features and details of the dolls that you make.

How to use the pattern graphs

The patterns for the dolls and their clothes will be found throughout the book drawn on squared grids; these are the pattern graphs. Before making a doll it is necessary to enlarge the pattern graph to full size. Careful pattern-making is essential. To make the enlargement you will need large sheets of paper marked with a grid where every square equals 2.5cm (1in). Paper already marked with a grid may be purchased either from stationers or haberdashery departments, but you can also make your own. It is well worth while making an accurate master copy and keeping this for all future doll-making. Patterns are then made by copying on to tracing paper laid over the master grid.

Copy the outline from the pattern graph in the book on to the corresponding squares on your ruled paper; this is called squaring up. If you are copying a large pattern piece it is helpful to number the squares both horizontally and vertically so that you can easily recognize reference points (see Fig 11). In many instances, where both sides of a pattern piece are the same, only half of it has been

Fig 11 Method of enlarging from pattern graph with reference points marked on the grid

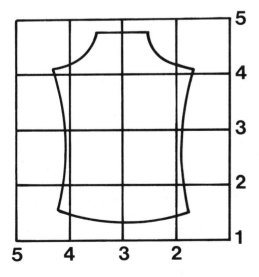

25

drawn on the pattern graph. Enlarge the half pattern and then lay edge marked 'fold' along the folded edge of another piece of paper and cut around the outline. Unfold the paper and you will have a full-size pattern piece. Paste the paper on to card to make a more permanent pattern.

Patterns for bodices, shirts and blouses have the same basic outline for both front and back so they have been drawn together on the pattern graph. Take care to copy the correct neckline and to add the extra width for the facing to either the centre front or the centre back. In just a few instances, where space is limited, dissimilar pattern pieces lie across one another. Again take care to copy the relevant piece when enlarging.

Pattern markings
As each pattern is made, transfer all information like back, front, arrow lines, number of pieces to be cut, centre front, darts and so on to full-size copy. The following conventions have been used:

Cutting line ————————————

Straight grain ———————————▶
    Place on fabric an even
    distance from selvedge

Stab stitching lines — — — — — —
    These are top-stitching
    lines, not seam lines

Guide-lines ••••••••••••••
    Position of elastic, ease
    and gathering threads

Clip ▲

Seam allowance: all patterns have a 6mm (¼in) allowance included unless otherwise stated.
Cut a pr: this means cut a pair so that you have a left and a right side. Turn the pattern over when cutting it out for the second time.

The dolls
Choice of fabric
The body of each doll has been designed for a particular fabric and the best results will be obtained by keeping to the fabric suggested or an equivalent substitute. Strong, firmly woven cotton materials like calico, poplin, gingham, sheeting and polyester and cotton mixtures have been used to make the majority of bodies. Choose a suitable flesh colour to suit the nationality of the doll, avoiding bright pinks or black wherever possible. In most instances, calico is the best choice. Wash fabrics first to remove dressing and to reduce the possibility of shrinking, then pull cloth into shape, dry and iron.

A popular fabric for making lightweight dolls, masks and for needle-modelling is stockinette. This varies both in width and in colour, the latter from pale flesh to bright apricot. The stockinette is manufactured as a tube with the stretch passing around the tube rather than along the length. It is useful for making short, plump dolls. Jersey and other similar knitted fabrics are possible alternatives.

26

Felt is a favourite material as it does not fray. It can be used to make small dolls either by stab stitching pieces together from the right side or by sewing narrow seams on the wrong side. You can also use felt to make successful face masks. There are several different thicknesses from paper-thin to a thick flooring quality, so take care when buying. Hold it up to the light and ensure that there are no thin patches. If you do have to strengthen the felt, either glue two layers together or back it with iron-on Vilene.

Humpty Dumpty and Rodriguez have parts of their bodies made from velvet and needlecord; both are fabrics with pile. Lay the patterns on the material and cut out so that the pile runs down the body and along the limbs towards the hands and feet.

Cutting out First press all fabrics, then lay pattern pieces on wrong side of folded fabric, making sure that the arrows are parallel to the selvedge. Felt may be cut in any direction so there are no arrows on patterns for this fabric. When cutting out stockinette, place patterns on fabric with the stretch going across the body from side to side. This usually means that the arrows lie parallel to the fold edges of the tube. Pin paper patterns in place or, if using card patterns, draw around the edge with a soft pencil.

Very small pattern pieces like the limbs for Gerry are best cut out as a block first and stitched inside the pencil line before cutting around the outline (see Fig 12). This technique is also used for the stockinette body of Bubbles and the hands of Cheko, as it reduces the chance of over-stretching the stockinette when sewing.

Fig 12 Block showing small pattern pieces stitched before cutting out

Seams Wherever possible the dolls should be stitched on a sewing machine and the seams of the bodies, in particular, should be stitched twice for extra strength. When sewing by hand, use a small, firm back stitch. Remember that 6mm (¼in) seams are included on the patterns. Use appropriate thread for the fabric, preferably one that has a certain amount of give in it so that the seams will not break during stuffing. Also use the correct size needle in your sewing machine.

Your machine will need adjusting to sew the stockinette. Reduce the pressure on the presser foot to stop the fabric spreading, use a fine needle or a ball-point needle and, if possible, a very shallow zigzag stitch. Gently stretch the seams as you sew to obtain the greatest elasticity. Again these seams need to be stitched twice.

Follow the instructions given for each doll, stitching body, head and limbs together in the correct sequence. Then trim all curves and clip corners before turning body skin right side out.

Stuffing and strengthening rods

Fig 13   Neck construction; (a) a wide continuous neck; (b) narrow continuous neck with additional strengthening provided by a dowel rod; (c) a wide end to end neck with head and body made separately; (d) end to end neck with a body extension and a dowel rod as additional strengthening; (e) neck formed by a body extension into head and (f) neck formed by a head extension into body and a strengthening dowel rod

The shape of a doll is determined primarily by the pattern and how efficiently it is stuffed. Simple dolls with head, body and limbs cut all-in-one have the stuffing continuous between all areas while more complex dolls have limbs and heads made and stuffed separately. The limbs and head are then hinged and sewn on to the body. The weakest part of any doll will generally be the neck, especially if it is thin and the proportions realistic. In these circumstances, additional support will be required to hold the head up. This support is usually provided by a strengthening rod, passed between the head and the body.

Figure 13 shows the six ways in which necks are constructed. The most popular strengthening rod is dowelling with a diameter of 12mm (½in), which is approximately the same thickness as your little finger. Other articles which are sometimes used include

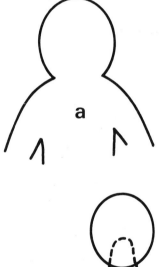

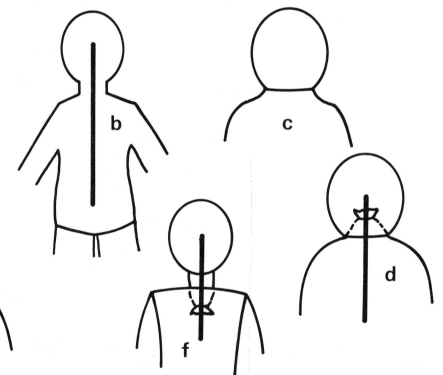

pencils, wooden spoons, plastic piping and even bound wire. All of these are placed in the dolls during stuffing and it is the way that you pack the stuffing around them that keeps the rod in position.

Dacron has been used as the stuffing for all the dolls in this book although kapok, terylene, polyester and cotton flock are all satisfactory alternatives. Your choice will probably be determined by availability and cost but do bear in mind that stuffings should be lightweight, washable and hygienic. Avoid using foam chips and cut-up nylons as these produce knobbly or heavy dolls. Both of these fillings are also coloured and may well show through the body skin thus spoiling the appearance of your work.

Stuffing is the bulking out of the body skin and needs considerable care. Prepare the stuffing fibre by teasing it apart and fluffing it out. Insert small wisps into the extremities of the skin, using long forceps or knitting needles to push the stuffing well down into hands and feet. Work consistently and patiently, continually turning the doll as you proceed, moulding limbs, checking for lumps or unfilled corners. Work back towards the opening, top stitching hinges as you come to them. Finally, close the opening with ladder stitch. Try and achieve firm, even stuffing except where a softer, less filled body is particularly called for — Bubbles is such an example. The success of your doll will depend on this stage, for without sufficient stuffing, heads will flop, joints will not work, limbs will wobble and clothes will not fit.

Dressmaking

Fabrics and trimmings Choose lightweight, firmly woven fabrics for dressmaking. These non-fraying fabrics will gather and drape more easily on the dolls and the seams will not need any special finishings. Prints, patterns and stripes should all be small and related to the size of the doll. Likewise lace, braids, ribbons and buttons should be the narrowest and smallest available. Embroidery can be used as an alternative to purchased trimmings. Unless otherwise stated, the fabric will always be 91cm (36in) wide.

Patterns for clothes Patterns are generally shown on the pattern graphs. Make full-size copies by following the instructions given for the dolls. However, some simple outline clothes, like the costumes for Cheko and Rebecca, are given as text figures. These figures contain all the necessary measurements to prepare a full-size copy. Garments that are made from shapes such as squares and circles are given as measurements in the text. Again, make full-size patterns. Because the patterns for clothes are given in several different places you must read through the complete instructions of the doll before cutting out. Only by doing this will you make sure that you have all the pieces required for the clothes.

Cutting out Press fabrics first then lay pattern on folded fabric, arrows parallel to selvedge. Pin pattern in place, or, if using a card pattern, draw around the outline of pieces that need to be cut double. To cut single pieces of pattern, open fabric out.

Making up Instructions for making the clothes are given with each doll but there are general points applicable to all dressmaking which it is more convenient to include here.

The clothes are designed for easy fitting, with gathered necks, sleeves and waists. In addition, many sleeves have elasticated wrists and there are pants with elasticated waists and leggings. However, it is still important to fit the clothes on the dolls as you make them.

The seams are generally machine-stitched while hems and finishings are hand sewn. All seams are 6mm (¼in) wide and are neatened by using a zigzag stitch or by trimming with pinking shears. Press, clip and trim seams as you work; this will ensure that you avoid any unnecessary puckering.

There are three different ways of putting elastic into garments. Firstly, using narrow elastic and a wide zigzag stitch, sew the elastic along the guide-line and at the same time stretch the elastic in front of the machine foot. Secondly, sew a bias binding casing on the inside of the garment and then thread with elastic. Lastly, wind shirring elastic on to a bobbin, lengthen the stitch and loosen the top tension, then sew from the right side of the garment.

The small size of the sleeves makes it virtually impossible to set them into an armhole in the conventional way, so the following method has been used throughout the book.

Prepare the bodice first by sewing front and back together on the shoulders only. On the sleeve run a gathering thread along the guide-line marked on the pattern, pull up thread, matching centre top of sleeve to shoulder seam and each side of sleeve to the outside edge of the armhole opening of the bodice. Baste in position, distributing the gathers evenly, then sew in place. Hem wrist edge then sew underarm seam and side seam of bodice or blouse in one continuous seam. Clip underarm corner.

Necks and armholes are difficult to finish neatly with collars and narrow hems. It is easier to use bias binding on these edges. Sew bias strip, with right side facing outside of garment, along the seam allowance line. Trim away excess fabric then fold binding over edge to inside of garment and hem in place on the machined line so that the stitches do not show on the finished garment. Sometimes it is more convenient to cut a facing or even a complete lining for a garment that has several edges to neaten. Details are given with the relevant dolls.

Fig 14 Methods of constructing bloomers, pants, knickers and pantaloons; (a) Continuous Strip method for making simple, short removable pants for flat dolls; (b) Outline Shape method for making long pants for flat dolls which are usually stitched permanently onto the body; (c) Shaped Crotch and Legs method for making bloomers. These have side seams in addition to the more usual centre front and centre back seams; (d) Square or Box method for making simple, long pants that are removable; (e) Shaped Crotch method for making shaped long pants that are easily removable

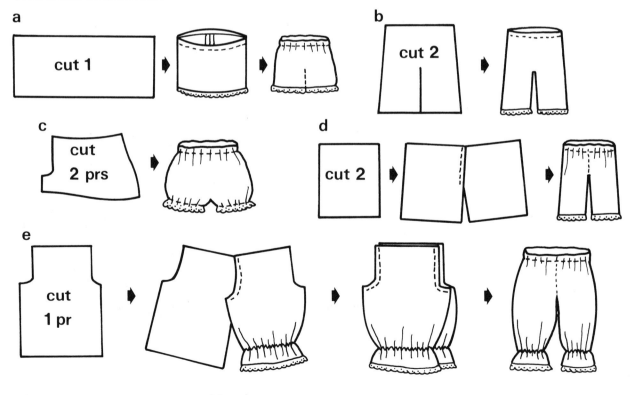

Bloomers, pants, knickers and pantaloons

Wherever possible, the dolls have removable pants. There are five basic styles of this undergarment and rather than repeat the instructions with every doll, they have been summarized here for easy reference. Figure 14 shows the various styles.

1. Join centre front seam and side seams, if any.
2. Make a narrow hem on leg edges.
3. Sew elastic across lower edge of each leg if required.
4. Join centre back seam.
5. Sew inside leg seam, breaking stitching at the crotch.
6. Fold down waist edge, make a channel, thread with elastic, fit on doll for size, fasten off and close opening.

Useful stitches

Ladder stitch is used for closing all openings on the body of a doll and for attaching the head securely to the body. To work ladder stitch you will need a strong needle and a double length of crochet cotton, which is generally stronger than cotton or linen threads. Make a small running stitch alternately on one side of the opening and then on the other and work from right to left (see Fig 15). After making a few stitches along the seam line, pull on the thread. It will lace up the opening, automatically turning in the raw edges to leave a smooth join.

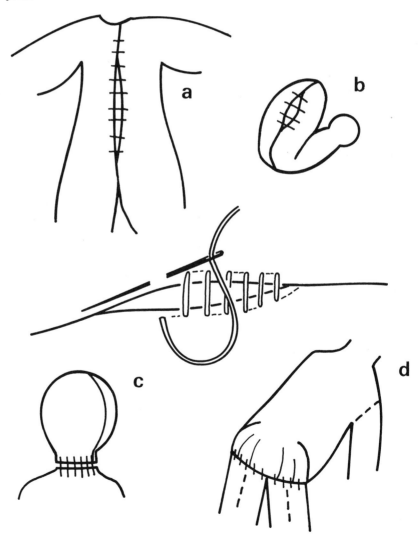

Fig 15 Ladder stitch and its uses; (a) for closing Cheko's costume; (b) closing body seams; (c) sewing head to body; (d) shaping a bottom by easing in the fullness at the back

Many of the dolls have embroidered faces or felt features that are applied with embroidery stitches. Figure 16 shows the stitches that are most frequently used and a few additional stitches that can be used to embroider hair on small dolls. Use three strands of embroidery thread and a fine, sharp needle. Start at the back of the head so that the knot will be hidden by the hair.

Fig 16   Useful embroidery stitches.
Top row, left to right stem, straight, chain and running stitches.
Middle row, left to right satin stitch, french knots and double crosses.
Bottom row, left to right laid stitch for making short hair and two stages of turkey stitch for making curls

Some embroidery stitches are also useful for making decorative trims on costumes when purchased braid would be too heavy. Feather stitch, pekinese, guilloche, raised chain band and double knot are examples for you to try. Instructions for working these stitches and many others may be found in most general embroidery books.

Plate 1   BODIES, ARMS AND LEGS
Left to right, seated Mandy, Miss Victoria, Wendy, Hilary, Norman
Foreground Rebecca

6 Flat dolls

A simple outline shape cut from a double layer of fabric produces a two-dimensional or flat doll. The stuffing provides the only depth as there are neither darts nor gussets for additional shaping and the resulting flatness is further emphasized by the absence of any limb articulation.

Three different methods are used to produce the various styled flat dolls of this chapter. For instance, The Butcher, The Baker and The Candlestick-maker are made in the style of printed fabric cut-outs. These cut-outs were much favoured by manufacturers in the United States as a means of advertising their products at the end of the nineteenth century. Even now, despite their limited play appeal, printed cut-outs are again enjoying a certain popularity. The recent development of fabric paints, crayons and textile pens has made it possible for anyone to draw or even trace a doll directly on to fabric and to paint in the features and clothes. It is a simple technique, producing distinctive and colourful dolls both quickly and inexpensively.

The second method of making flat dolls is based on the stump dolls of the sixteenth century. These were wooden dolls that had the head, arms and torso carved from a single piece of wood. Since the legs were to be hidden by clothing, the wood below the waist was simply left as an uncarved stump. This same principle can be used when making fabric dolls like Elizabeth and Erika.

The last method utilizes the readily recognizable universal 'stick figure' representation of the human form. Almost any drawing of a stick figure can be padded out to a suitable thickness, ready for making a pattern. Indeed, it is this simple method that frequently provides the basis for more complex dolls. Allowances or even separate pieces can be added to the basic pattern for shaping and limbs can be made to articulate in a number of specific ways.

The Butcher, the Baker, the Candlestick-maker

Height: 35 to 40cm (14 to 16in)
Plate 2; pattern graph 1

Fabric paints have been used to decorate these three jolly nursery-rhyme characters. Paints generally give brighter colours than crayons and in addition have a greater number of basic colours, including black and white. They can also be used for much finer detail than crayons. It is important to read the manufacturer's instructions carefully before proceeding, as some fabric colours can only be used on natural fibres such as cotton and linen, while others

Plate 2 FLAT DOLLS
Top Girls and Boys;
Centre, left to right Katrina, The Baker, The Candlestick-maker, The Butcher;
Bottom, left to right Erika, Elizabeth, two Girls and Boys

front
cut 1

back
cut 1

seam line

Pattern graph 1   1 square = 2.5cm (1in)

require synthetic fibres such as nylon, crimplene and even Vilene. Flesh tinting for Vilene is achieved by dyeing the fabric in the appropriate cold-water dye first. When the Vilene is dry it can be coloured with fabric crayons. Most methods of fabric colouring are made colourfast by heat treatment, a very necessary precaution if the dolls are to be washed.

Materials for dolls   1m (1yd) of washed and ironed calico; 454g (1lb) stuffing; Dylon Color; fun fabric paint in assorted colours; black waterproof marker such as a Tempo or Scripto pen.

The dolls   *Body:*   The pattern given is that for the Baker. Use this pattern to make the other two characters, altering the hat shape to make either a boater or a top hat as required. Beware of making narrow brims.

Lay the pattern pieces on calico and draw round the outline. Do not cut out at this stage. Instead, cut the front and back into two blocks of fabric. They will be easier to paint and handle in this way. Mark in the seam allowance and outline of clothes with a soft pencil.

Follow the maker's directions for using and mixing the paints.

Begin by painting the skin with a flesh tone, then all the white clothes. The eyes are also easier to do if you paint them completely white now. Allow the paint to dry between applications of different colours. Continue by painting the hair, shoes, French loaf, wooden spoon, and so on.

Use the black pen to mark in the outlines of fingers, eyes, clothes, creases in the hat, pupils and the moustache. Use the tip of your little finger to blush the cheeks by rubbing in a small amount of red paint. When the paint is completely dry, iron the fabric to fix the colour.

Cut out the front and back body, place them right sides together and sew around the outline, leaving an opening at the base. Turn the body over to the other side and re-sew the outline. The paint is visible through the calico and by stitching the doll from both sides you should eliminate the need to touch up along the seam line with more paint. Clip corners, turn right side out and stuff. Close the opening. To stop wrinkles appearing at the neck, form a crease at the back between the clothes and head. Do this by running your little finger back and forth from side to side. Work a row of ladder stitch across what is effectively a surface-made dart. Additional shaping can be given to the doll by taking a stitch right through the midline at the bottom of the trousers. This will also prevent stuffing from moving in and out of the shoes.

The Butcher   Look carefully at the colour illustration (Plate 2) before making a pattern. He wears a traditional boater hat and striped apron. In front he holds a large carving knife while a back view would show a string of sausages. To paint the curls, make a series of swirls. When dry, outline some of the swirls with the black marker.

The Candlestick-maker   Again, look carefully at the colour illustration before making a pattern. He is painted wearing a black top hat and jacket with tails while his trousers are purple. The clothes are protected by an apron. In front he carries a burning candle while behind, his hand holds a silver candle-snuffer.

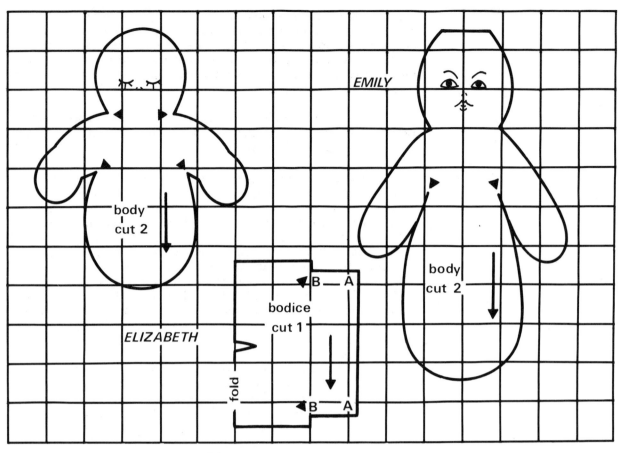

Pattern graph 2

1 square = 2.5cm (1in)

Elizabeth

Length: 30cm (12in)
Plate 2; pattern graph 2

Elizabeth is a fabric stump doll, dressed as an infant would have been approximately 100 years ago and made to lie on a satin pillow. The long dresses of these infants usually had short sleeves and elaborately decorated front panels. Favourite colours for satin ribbons were yellow, blue, pink and even red. Elizabeth's dress and bonnet are not removable.

Materials for doll   30.5cm (12in) square of calico; 28g (1oz) stuffing; embroidery threads for face; colouring for cheeks.

Materials for clothes   25cm (¼yd) fine white fabric for dress; 1m (1yd) narrow white satin ribbon; 33cm (13in) of 38mm (1½in) wide white satin ribbon for bonnet; 30.5cm (12in) double-edged lace for front panel; narrow lace to trim edge of sleeves and front edge of bonnet.

Materials for pillow   30.5cm (12in) by 46cm (18in) white satin or taffeta; 28g (1oz) stuffing; 1m (1yd) lace; 50cm (½yd) narrow white ribbon to hold doll in place; press stud.

The doll   *Body:*   Sew front and back body pieces together, leaving an opening at the top of the head. Clip underarms and turn right side out. Stuff and then close opening.
Facial features: Work all the features with three strands of embroidery thread. The eyes are outlined in stem stitch while the eyelashes and nostrils are small straight stitches. Blush the cheeks with either lipstick or pencil.
Hair: The curls on the forehead are a cluster of approximately 18 french knots.

The clothes   *Dress:*   Cut bodice and a skirt measuring 23cm (9in) long by 53cm (21in) wide from fine white fabric. It may be necessary to cut a lining for the skirt if a sheer fabric is being used. Hem wrist edges of sleeves and trim with narrow lace. Fold bodice in half across the shoulders and sew each underarm seam from A to B. Slit centre back of bodice up to neck opening and make a single hem round the neck. Sew short sides of skirt together, leaving a 5cm (2in) opening at the waist edge. Gather waist to fit bodice then sew together. Hem skirt. Hand-sew double-edged lace to front of dress, making the centre panel. Fit dress on doll and close back opening from neck to below the waist. Make a satin bow and stitch it to the waist at the front.
Bonnet: Hem both short edges of the wide satin ribbon and sew narrow lace to one long edge. This will be the front of the bonnet. Now work 4 rows of evenly spaced gathers along the length of the ribbon as shown in Figure 17. Pull up gathers on the crown as tightly as possible and on the other rows slightly less tightly so that the front edge will frame the face. Sew the short edges together for 8mm at the crown. Place bonnet on Elizabeth and sew in place with satin ribbon, making a bow under the chin.

Fig 17 Elizabeth's bonnet, showing position of gathering stitches and back view of finished bonnet

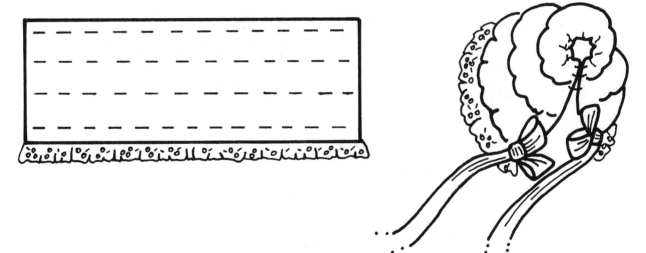

The pillow   Cut a double cushion shape to fit the dressed infant. Round it off at the top but leave the bottom as a straight edge. Seam together, leaving the base open. Turn right side out and lightly stuff. Close the opening. Sew gathered lace to the edge of the pillow. Make two ribbon rosettes with ties and sew one to each end of a 17cm (7in) length of ribbon. To find the exact position for this holding ribbon lay Elizabeth on the pillow and place the ribbon over the waist and under the arms. Sew one rosette firmly to the pillow and attach the second rosette to the other side of the pillow by means of a press stud.

Erika

Length: 20cm (8in)
Plate 2; pattern graph 2

Erika is another fabric stump infant but in contrast to Elizabeth, she wears a much shorter, coloured dress and a removable knitted matinée jacket with matching bonnet. These are the clothes of a present-day infant. The colour illustration shows Erika lying in an oval bread basket which has been lined and furnished with a pillow to make a baby's bed.

Materials for doll   These are the same as given for Elizabeth, p 38.

Materials for clothes   15cm (6in) by 91cm (36in) baby-pink patterned fabric; 28g (1oz) 4-ply pink wool; 3¼mm (no 10) knitting needles; 50cm (½yd) narrow pink ribbon.

The doll   Make the doll by following the instructions given for Elizabeth.

The clothes   *Dress:*   Cut the skirt of the dress to measure 39cm (15in) wide by 13cm (5in) long. Make up as described for Elizabeth, gathering wrist edge on to arms and omitting all the lace trimmings.
Matinée jacket: Cast on 60 stitches and knit 22 rows of garter stitch. Cast off tightly. Thread narrow pink ribbon between stitches just below the cast-off edge. Following Figure 18, top-stitch for 12mm (½in) through both thicknesses of knitting on each side to form the sleeves.
Bonnet: Cast on 27 stitches and knit 18 rows of garter stitch. Cast off tightly. Gather up cast-off edge and join both ends together to form the crown. Sew a short centre back seam, down from the crown. Sew bonnet on to Erika or make a ribbon tie.

Fig 18   Erika's matinee jacket, showing position of top stitching to form the sleeves

Emily

Height: 20cm (8in)
Plate 6; pattern graph 2

This is a fabric stump doll of more mature proportions. The clothes are sewn in place to the body and by making frills around the hemline it is possible for the doll to stand. If necessary, a Vilene petticoat cone would provide additional support for standing.

Materials for doll   30.5cm (12in) square of calico; 56g (2oz) stuffing; approximately 10m (½oz) double knitting wool for hair; black felt-tip pen.

Materials for clothes   15cm (6in) small-print cotton; scrap of ribbon for the neck; 4 small beads.

The doll   *Body:* Sew front and back body together, leaving the top of the head open. Clip corners, turn right side out and stuff. Close opening.
Hair: Wind the wool approximately 40 times around a card template to make a 13cm (5in) long hank. Do not cut the loops formed at either end. Machine a 5cm (2in) wide centre parting and stitch the hair on to the head through this parting. Catch the loops down at the nape of the neck, evenly distributing them around the sides and back of the head.
Facial features: Draw in the features with a felt-tip pen.

The clothes   *Dress:* Cut skirt measuring 15cm (6in) long by 40cm (16in) wide and then cut the remainder of the print into 5cm (2in) wide strips. Sew short sides of skirt together to make a centre back seam. Hem the bottom edge. Cut sufficient material from one of the strips to make two sleeves. Hem the wrist edges then sew each sleeve into a tube. Turn sleeves right side out and position on each arm. Cut the head of each sleeve so that the outside sits on the shoulder and can be stitched to the doll.

Hem both edges of remaining strips and gather up to make two frills, one for the bottom of the skirt and a smaller one for the bodice. Sew a small piece of ribbon to cover the chest of the doll then arrange the bodice frill to come over the shoulders from front to back. Sew in place so that the frill hides the top of the sleeves and the edge of the ribbon. Sew the small beads on the ribbon to act as buttons.

Sew the longer frill to the hem of the skirt then gather the waist edge to fit the doll and sew in place. The gathers should be hidden by the bodice frill and the skirt should be long enough to allow the doll to stand.

Lavender Lil

Height: 20cm (8in)
Plate 6

Lavender Lil, as her name implies, is a lavender-scented stump doll. She would make a rather unusual sachet to put amongst the linen and by adding a loop she could be made to hang in a wardrobe.

Materials for doll   These are the same as for Emily with the addition of a few teaspoons of dried lavender.

Materials for clothes   15cm (6in) by 40cm (16in) of small-check, lavender-coloured gingham; 2.25m (7ft) similar coloured lace; ribbon backing for the lace, optional.

The doll   Make as for Emily but sprinkle the dried lavender amongst the stuffing in the stump of the doll.

The clothes   *Dress:* Make skirt as for Emily. Cut two 61cm (24in) lengths of lace. Gather each length and sew to the hem line making a double flounce. Cut two 10cm (4in) lengths of lace. Gather each length and sew one to each arm as a sleeve. Divide the remaining lace into two lengths, gather and sew to the doll around the neck and over the shoulders. This double tier makes the bodice.

Katrina

Height: 45cm (18in)
Plate 2; pattern graph 3

Katrina is a simple shaped stick doll with hands and feet left as rounded off ends to the limbs. She wears the costume of an Eastern European lass yet manages to capture a certain gypsy flavour. The clothes have been made with elasticated waists or neck making them easy to pull on or off. Katrina is the only dressable flat doll.

Materials for doll   50cm (½yd) calico; 227g (8oz) stuffing; 20cm (8in) wooden dowel; 28g (1oz) double knitting wool; black felt for eyes; brown and white Sylko; colouring for cheeks.

Materials for clothes   24cm (9½in) by 56cm (22in) black crimplene; assorted braids, ribbon and ricrac to decorate the skirt; 2 gold rings; 30.5cm (12in) square of black felt; 6 gold beads for boot buttons; 40cm (16in) green taffeta for blouse and pants; 70cm (27in) narrow elastic; small pieces of felt and ribbon to make the head-dress.

The doll   *Body:*   Sew front and back body together leaving the top of the head open. Clip corners, especially the top of the legs, turn right side out and stuff. Remember to insert the dowel rod. Close the opening on top of the head by folding over both sets of opposite sides as you would do when wrapping up a box parcel. Stitch flaps down.
Hair: Wind wool into a 43cm (17in) hank. Cut loops at both ends and sew a 9cm (3½in) wide central parting. Attach the hair to the doll by sewing through the parting. Glue down the hair at the back after sewing the head-dress in place.
Facial features: Cut two, 15mm (⅝in) diameter circles of black felt for the eyes. Embroider small triangles of white straight stitches for highlights then hem the eyes in place and work a few brown straight stitches on upper edge for eyelashes. Work two more straight stitches for the nostrils. Rub colouring into the cheeks.

The clothes   *Pants:*   Cut two pieces of material 18cm (7in) wide by 25cm (10in) long. Follow instructions for Square method construction of pants in the Dressmaking section, page 30, sewing a 12cm (5in) centre front and back seam.
Blouse: Cut one of the blouse pieces along the fold line to make a centre back opening. Now sew each side of the back to the front blouse along the upper sleeve edge from wrist to neck. Hem wrist edges. Sew a continuous underarm seam on each side from wrist to waist. Hem back opening on both sides and the waist line. Fold down the neck edge and sew a hem wide enough to act as a casing for the elastic. Remember to clip the seam between the neck and shoulder seam. Thread elastic through the neck. Work fastenings on the back of the blouse.

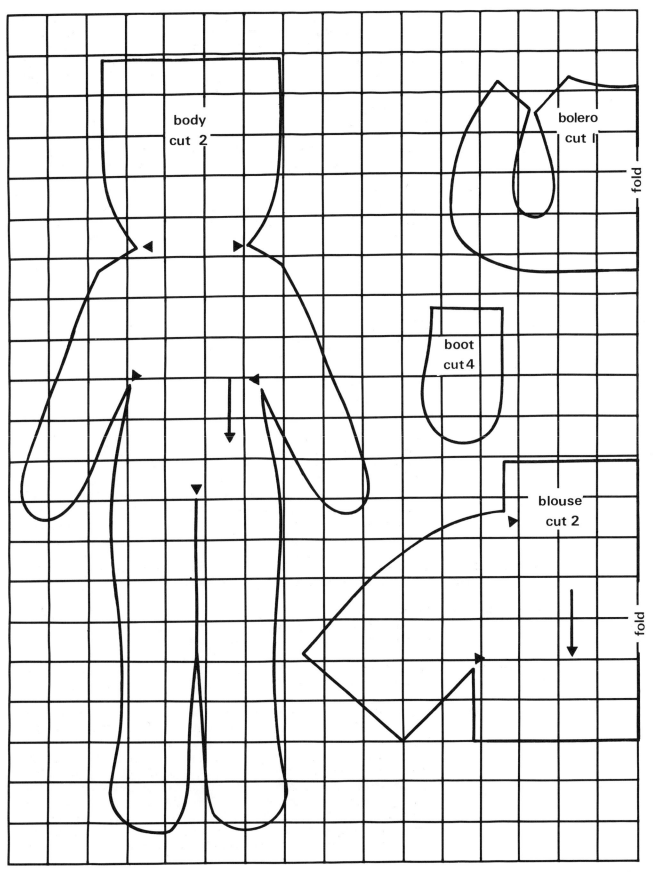

body
cut 2

bolero
cut 1

fold

boot
cut 4

blouse
cut 2

fold

Pattern graph 3

1 square = 2.5cm (1in)

Skirt: Cut skirt fabric in half lengthways so that you have two pieces, each measuring 24cm (9½in) by 28cm (11in). Shape both sides of each piece by cutting up at an angle from the 28cm lower hem edge to make a 23cm (9in) upper waist edge. Now sew both side seams of the skirt, hem lower edge and decorate with braid and ribbon. Make a hem along the waist edge that is wide enough to thread through elastic.

Bolero: Cut as one piece from black felt. Sew the narrow shoulder seams then decorate with ricrac or peasant-style embroidery.

Boots: Cut from black felt. Hand-sew each boot together on the right side. Fit on to doll and hold firmly in place by sewing three beads on to each boot, making sure that the stitches pass into the calico beneath the felt.

Head-dress: Sew a piece of fancy braid on to the head in place of a head band. Decorate the sides with small felt flowers made from scraps and ribbon streamers. Sew rings in place for ear-rings.

Girls and Boys

Height: 18cm (7in)
Plate 2; pattern graph 4

'Girls and boys come out to play' was what I had in mind when designing these small stick-figure flat dolls. Children love arranging and rearranging dolls in all sorts of groups, like family, friends and schools. They will often sit for long spells playing quietly at the make-believe games, telling the dolls what to do. Collecting them all together in their own bag means that they should stay together and of course be easy to carry about. The amount of time and patience that you will need to make these dolls will surely be well rewarded.

Materials for making all six dolls
50cm (½yd) calico; 170g (6oz) stuffing; embroidery thread for features; small amounts of 4-ply wool for the hair.

Materials for clothes
Remnants of small-print cottons to make dress and pants for girls; needlecord for trousers; satin for shirts; narrow lace and ribbon to trim as required; embroidery thread for shoes.

Materials for bag
60cm (23in) needlecord; 19cm (7½in) diameter circle of foam and the same again of stiff card; 75cm (30in) cord for drawstring.

The dolls
Body: Sew front and back body together leaving the top of the head open. Turn right side out, stuff and close the opening. The top of the head is folded in as described for Katrina, page 42.

Hair: All the girls have plaits. These are made by cutting 32 strands of 30.5cm (12in) long wool. Back stitch the wool on to the head in the position of a centre parting. Pull wool down firmly to the nape of the neck and again catch in place. Divide wool into two equal bundles and make a plait with each. Trim the ends. The hair for the boys is made by working several rows of laid stitch. The front row frames the face with shorter stitches to the side while two or even

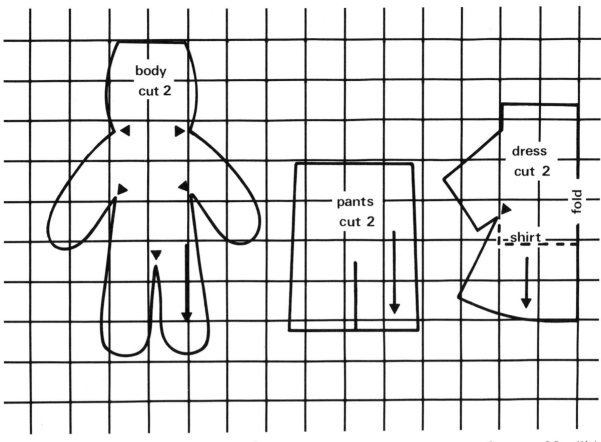

Pattern graph 4   1 square = 2.5cm (1in)

three rows cover the back of the head. Keep working until all the calico is covered.

Facial features: The eyes are outlined and filled in with pale blue stem stitch. Use dark blue or dark brown to work satin-stitch pupils. Work straight stitches to make the eyelashes and nostrils. The girls have pink cheeks of double cross stitch and mouths of two small straight stitches.

The clothes   *Shoes:* Embroider the shoes for both sexes, using laid stitch. Work an ankle strap of chain stitch in the front for the girls.

Pants: The pants for both girl and boy dolls are made in the same way. Follow the instructions for the Outline method in the Dressmaking section, page 30. The waist edge is gathered directly on to the dolls, but do remember to tuck in the boy's shirt before sewing down.

Dress: Sew outer sleeve seam from the wrist up to the neck edge. Hem wrist and decorate with lace. Sew underarm and side seam of dress. Clip corners. Make a narrow hem at the bottom of the dress. Fit dress on doll by feeding the feet through the neck opening. Turn under the neck edge and gather to fit the doll. Stitch narrow ribbon around the waist as a belt.

Shirt: Use the upper portion of the dress pattern to cut out the shirt. Make as for the dress but omit the lace trim on the sleeves. Make a collar of gathered lace.

The bag   Cut needlecord into a strip measuring 60cm (23in) by 68cm (27in) and from the remainder cut two circles, each having a diameter of 23cm (9in). One circle is for the base, the other will be used to cover the card stiffener.

45

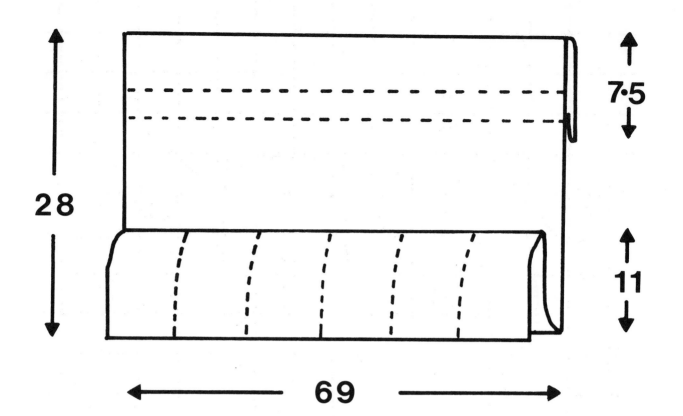

28

7·5

11

69

Fig 19   Construction of bag for Girls and Boys. Measurements given in centimetres. (7.5cm = 3in; 11cm = 4½in; 28cm = 11in; 69cm = 27in)

Follow the measurements given in Figure 19 and fold up the lower edge of the needlecord to form the pocket strip. Top stitch through all three thicknesses making six equally spaced slots for the dolls. Now sew the two short sides of the bag together on the wrong side. Fold down the top edge and stitch a double row to make a channel for the drawcord. Sew circle base in position. Make this seam really secure by double stitching.

Form two small slits in the channel on the outside of the bag. One slit should lie on the side seam and the other will be directly opposite it on the other side of the bag. Work buttonhole stitch around the slits then thread in a double loop of drawcord, fastening the ends together securely.

Lay the circle of foam on top of the circle of card. Cover both with the remaining circle of needlecord by running a gathering stitch around the edge. Place the lining in the bottom of the bag with the card against the base. You are now ready to put a doll in each pocket.

Some more ideas for flat dolls

1. Make a tub to hold The Butcher, The Baker and The Candlestick-maker.

2. Paint portrait dolls or caricatures of your family, friends and favourite personalities.

3. Add embroidery stitches to embellish painted cut-outs.

4. Instead of painting the dolls, try some other techniques like machine embroidery, free style embroidery, appliqué, quilting, patchwork, either separately or combining them.

5. Make cut-outs large enough to be cushions.

6. Elizabeth can be made as a 'turnabout' doll, asleep one side and wide awake the other. Keep the unwanted face covered by a bonnet and make a removable dress so that it can always be turned front-wards to the appropriate face.

7. Dress the stump infant in a barrow coat and make a Baby Bunting by adding ears to a hood.

8. Re-draw the stump on Emily as a mermaid's tail. Make up the doll and cover the tail with scale-like stitches or rows of ricrac.

9. Use the stump dolls as a basic shape to make a series of costume dolls.

10. Make a fabric shoe large enough to hold several Girls and Boys. Then make a mother doll and you have the 'Old Woman who Lived in a Shoe'.

7 Hinged dolls

Many of the flat dolls of the previous chapter can be used as a basis for making dolls that bend their limbs and can be sat down. As soon as the relevant sections are stuffed, they are sewn off, providing an unstuffed hinge area that allows the fabric to bend and twist both forwards and backwards at these points. These swinging, stitched hinges were one of the earliest forms of articulation devised for commercially made cloth dolls in the middle of the nineteenth century. They are just as popular today with manufacturers and home doll-makers. Bodies that have hinges at the hips and shoulders only are referred to as single-hinged dolls while those that have additional hinges at the knees and elbows are referred to as double-hinged dolls.

The disadvantage of continuing to use outline, shaped, flat doll patterns for hinging is that the heads lack shape and depth and that the feet invariably face the wrong way. By cutting the limbs separately, especially the legs, it is possible to sew them into the body seams at the hips and shoulders and form the hinge at the same time. A separately constructed head also allows greater freedom in design.

Bubbles is a lightly stuffed, single-hinged doll that is very floppy and cuddly. She has been developed from a flat-doll pattern. Hilary is a firmly stuffed single-hinged doll that has legs cut separately from the rest of the body. Rodriguez is a single-hinged doll that has stuffed clothing in place of separate limbs. The shoulder hinge of this doll is formed by lapping the arm on to the body. Arabella, the last doll of the chapter, is a double-hinged doll. The easy movement that goes with the additional hinges is particularly suitable for a long legged doll. It also makes the doll very easy to dress and undress, thereby greatly increasing the play value.

Bubbles

Height: 33cm (13in)
Plate 3; pattern graph 5

The pattern for this doll resembles the simple cut-out shapes of the previous chapter but because it is made from stockinette the doll can be softly sculptured. Furthermore, the feet can be bent forward at right angles to the body and stitched in place to the legs. The resulting contours, with the addition of hinges, produce a doll that is far from flat. Stockinette is not easy to work with because it stretches out of shape so easily. Begin making Bubbles by reading the instructions for working with stockinette first (see p 27).

Materials for doll   46cm (18in) stockinette cut from a tube 53cm (21in) wide; 56g (2oz)

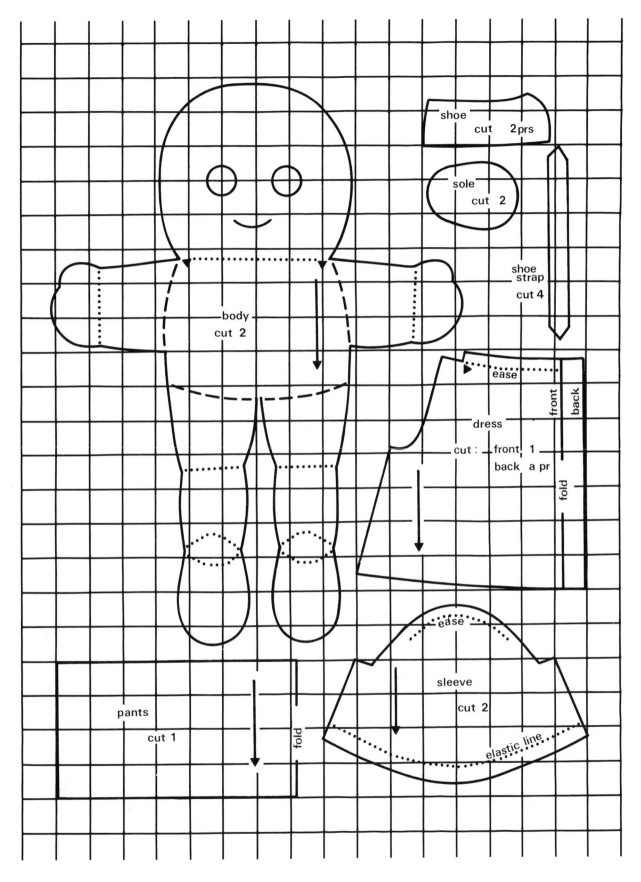

shoe
cut 2prs

sole
cut 2

shoe
strap
cut 4

body
cut 2

ease

front back

dress

cut: front 1
back a pr

fold

ease

sleeve
cut 2

elastic line

pants
cut 1

fold

fold

Pattern graph 5

1 square = 2.5cm (1in)

double knitting wool for hair; 56g (2oz) stuffing; felt for eyes; embroidery thread for mouth; cheek colouring.

Materials for clothes   30.5cm (⅓yd) printed cotton; 107cm (42in) lace trim, optional; snap fasteners; 30.5cm (12in) narrow elastic; 23cm (9in) square of felt for shoes; two small buttons; one pair first size baby socks.

The doll   *Body:*   Lay the pattern on doubled stockinette and draw around the body with a soft pencil. Do not cut out just yet. Instead, machine front and back body pieces together just inside the pencilled line leaving the top of the head open. This stops the stockinette from slipping and stretching while you sew. Now cut along the pencil line and clip into tight corners. Turn body right side out and commence stuffing.

Legs: Stuff the feet and legs first. Bend each foot forward in turn and ladder stitch to the front of the leg. The stitches should bring the two curved lines of the pattern together, thus effectively working a curved dart from the right side. Look at the foot critically and decide whether it needs to be pulled up further. This will depend very much on how you stuff the doll.

When satisfied with the position, work a row of small running stitches across the back of the ankle to give more shaping if so desired. Work another row of running stitches across the back of the knee. The hip hinge is made by sewing a row of running stitches through all thicknesses across the top of the legs. Pull up on the stitches so that the legs stay together and do not splay apart.

Arms: Stuff the arms, being very careful not to stretch them, then work a row of running stitches down from the neck to the armpit on each side to form the shoulder hinges. Work a row of small running stitches across the front of each wrist.

Head: The head and body proper can now be stuffed as a single unit. Work a row of gathering stitches around the neck and draw up so that the neck has a circumference of 16.5cm (6½in). When the head is correctly stuffed, it should measure 28cm (11in) around on a line level with the eyes. Close opening on top of head.

Facial features: Cut felt into two round pupils. Embroider a small white triangular highlight on each eye then hem in position. Work eyelashes with dark-coloured straight stitches and mouth with rose-coloured stem stitch. Blush cheeks with colouring very slowly and carefully.

Hair: Wind wool on to a 5cm (2in) wide Quadframe or template. Stitch through centre so that curls are 2.5cm (1in) deep on either side of the stitching. Make strips of curls until all the wool is used up. Arrange curls on head to frame the face first then spirally to cover the back of the head. Back stitch in place through base of the curls. Alternatively stitch loops on to the head with a finer thread as wool will not pass easily through the stockinette.

The clothes   *Pants:*   Make up the pants by following directions for the Continuous Strip method (p 30). Decorate the leg edge with lace. Separate the leg openings by top-stitching through the centre front to the back for a short distance.

Dress: Sew backs to front at the shoulders so far as the clip mark. Ease up the head of each sleeve with a gathering thread then fit into respective armholes. Adjust the gathers and then sew sleeve in position. Hem wrist edges and decorate with lace. Work a row of gathers or a line of elastic 12mm (½in) back from the wrist. Join each underarm seam and side of dress in one continuous seam. Neaten

Plate 3   HINGED DOLLS
Top, left to right Harry, Rodriguez, Rodney;
Centre, left to right Bubbles, Hinemoa, Arabella;
Bottom Hilary

50

back opening and gather up neck edge to fit doll. Finish neck with a bias strip and add lace to decorate. Hem dress and sew snap fasteners down the back opening.

Socks: Fit socks on to feet, reshape the toe by trimming away the excess sock and making a new seam.

Shoes: Sew a pair of felt shoe pieces together at the toe and heel. Insert sole, matching fullness to the front. Glue two strap pieces together then, when dry, sew a row of machine or stab stitching all along the edge. Join strap to heel of shoe. Sew a button on one end and cut a slit on the other end of the strap. Remember to make the shoes as a pair. Decorate each shoe with a felt flower or a small felt twist.

Hilary

Height: 40cm (16in)
Plates 1 and 3; pattern graph 6

This is a very quick and simple doll to make. It is basically the same pattern as that used for Bubbles but here the legs have been constructed separately so that no needle-modelling is needed to bring the feet forward. The body should be stuffed very firmly, especially the neck, to prevent the head from flopping over.

Materials for doll   25cm (10in) calico; 170g (6oz) stuffing; 18cm (7in) dowelling, 12mm (½in) diameter; 28g (1oz) double knitting wool for hair; embroidery threads for face; colouring for cheeks.

Materials for clothes   30.5cm (⅓yd) cotton for dress and pants; 50cm (20in) narrow elastic; snap fasteners for dress; small piece of white cotton for apron; optional lace trim and ricrac; ribbon for hair bows; 15cm (6in) square of felt for shoes; button for apron.

The doll   *Legs:* Sew legs together in pairs, leaving the top open. Turn right side out and stuff as far as the line marked on the pattern. Press top of each leg flat so that seams meet in the centre. Baste edges together.

Body: Sew front and back body pieces together leaving an opening on top of the head and again across the bottom straight edge. Turn right side out. Turn in seam allowance at base of body and insert tops of legs, toes facing forwards, and stitch across. Stuff each arm, then make the shoulder hinges by working a row of running stitches from neck to armpit on each side. Finish stuffing body and head, enclosing the dowel rod in the middle of the doll. Close opening.

Facial features: Embroider the pupils with solid stem stitch and the outline of the eye with a row of stem stitch and work straight-stitch eyelashes. The mouth is also worked in stem stitch while the cheeks are blushed with either lipstick or red pencil.

Hair: Wind the wool into a 20cm (8in) hank. Cut loops at one end only so that wool opens out to strands 41cm (16in) long. Sew a centre parting 14cm (5½in) wide. Place hair on doll and sew to head through the parting. Catch hair down on each side, level with the

Plate 4   JOINTED DOLLS
Left to right Mandy, Cheko the Clown, Miss Victoria

53

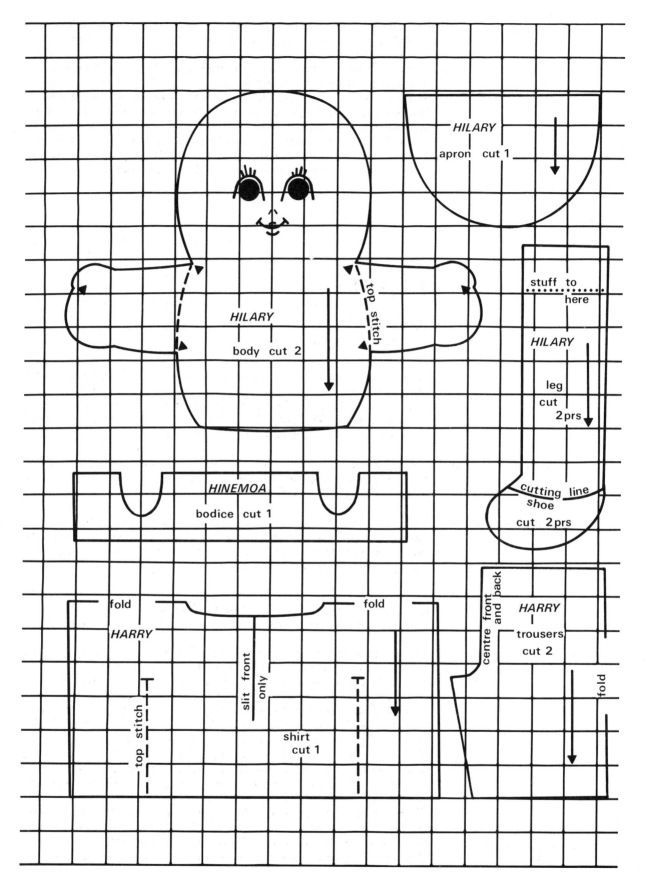

HILARY

apron cut 1

stuff to here

HILARY

leg cut 2 prs

HILARY

body cut 2

top stitch

cutting line shoe cut 2 prs

HINEMOA

bodice cut 1

fold

fold

HARRY

top stitch

slit front only

shirt cut 1

centre front and back

HARRY

trousers cut 2

fold

Pattern graph 6

1 square = 2.5cm (1in)

ears to make two bunches. Tie the ribbon into two bows and sew one to each bunch.

The clothes *Pants:* Follow the pattern for Bubbles and cut the pants so that they are 14cm (5½in) deep. This makes them longer than those of Bubbles, which allows you to sew a hem along the leg edge to hold elastic. Apart from this, the pants are made in the same way as those for Bubbles.

Dress: This also uses the pattern given for Bubbles but in this instance cut the dress slightly longer. Follow the instructions given for Bubbles and finish by decorating the hem with Broderie Anglaise.

Apron: Decorate the curved edge of the apron skirt with Broderie Anglaise and ricrac sewn on to a narrow hem. Gather up the straight edge slightly. Now cut a waistband measuring 4cm (1½in) by 30.5cm (12in). Sew apron skirt to centre edge of waistband with right sides together. Fold waistband in half, again with right sides together, and sew the two short sides and along to the edge of the skirt. Turn waistband straps right side out. Slip stitch opening closed. Sew button on to one end of strap and work a buttonhole opening on the other end. See Figure 20.

Shoes: Sew felt sides together in pairs. Turn right side out and fit a shoe on to each foot and slip stitch in place.

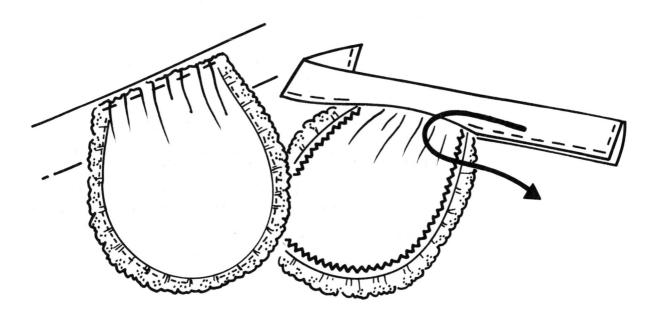

Fig 20   Construction of apron for Hilary showing how waistband is attached and then turned right side out

Hinemoa

Height: 40cm (16in)
Plate 3; pattern graph 6

Hinemoa is a variation of Hilary, made as a Maori maiden. Legend has it that Hinemoa and Tu had been forbidden to marry by her parents. Despite this, she left her village by the shore and swam across the lake one dark night, guided by the sound of Tu playing his flute from the island.

Materials for doll Choose a warm brown cotton in place of the calico; you will also need 50g (2oz) of black mohair wool for the hair.

Materials for clothes 30.5cm (12in) by 5cm (2in) black felt for bodice (pari); 30.5cm (12in) by 15cm (6in) red cotton for underskirt; garden raffia for skirt (piupiu); small quantity of black, red and white wool; small piece of red felt.

The doll *Body:* Follow directions for Hilary.
Facial features: Work the face as for Hilary but embroider brown eyes and fill in the space on either side with white stem stitch. Outline the eyes with dark-brown stem stitch. Use a biscuit colour for the mouth and omit the cheeks.
Hair: Wind mohair into a 40cm (16in) hank. Cut loops at both ends. Sew a centre parting then lay hair on head and sew securely in place. Hold hair down with a thin layer of glue. Trim to size as necessary.

The clothes *Headband (tipare):* Plait all the red, black and white wool together until you have about 2m (2yd) of braid. Wind a small length of braid around the forehead and stitch in place.
Skirt (piupiu): Look at Figure 21 and follow the diagram for constructing the ceremonial costume. Hem both sides and bottom edge of underskirt. Cut raffia to required length and sew across top edge of waistline of underskirt. Mark black lines on raffia by laying a ruler down and drawing across it with a black felt-tip pen. Sew skirt to the bodice.
Bodice (pari): Cut a diamond shape from the red felt and place it centrally on the bodice. Lay the braid down in a symmetrical pattern and hem in place. Make straps of wool to reach over armholes. Attach two snap fasteners to the back opening.
Tiki: A small plastic tiki has been hung around the neck; make one from painted card or self-hardening clay.

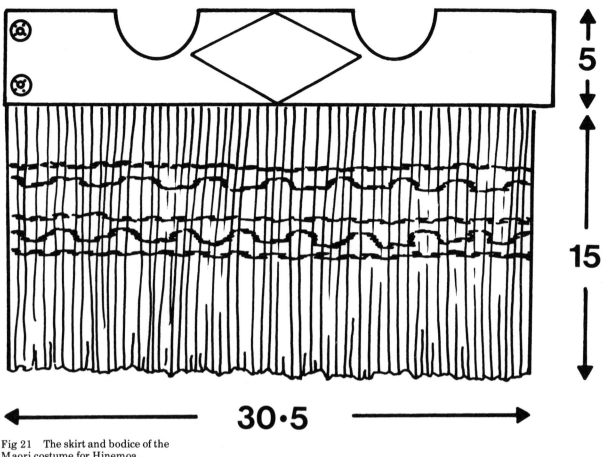

Fig 21   The skirt and bodice of the Maori costume for Hinemoa. Measurements given in centimetres. (5cm = 2in; 15cm = 6in; 30.5cm = 12in)

Harry

Height: 40cm (16in)
Plate 3; pattern graph 6

Harry is a male version of Hilary. He is very much a young East African lad, dressed in bright colours.

Materials for doll   Choose a dark-brown cotton for the body; you will also need 40g (1½oz) of black poodle wool for the hair.

Materials for clothes   28cm (11in) square bright cotton for shirt; 1m (1yd) bias binding for shirt; 23cm (9in) striped cotton for trousers; elastic for waist.

The doll   *Body:*   Make as for Hilary.
Facial features: Work as for Hinemoa but keep whites of eyes to one side only.
Hair: Cover the head with short curls.

The clothes   *Shirt:*   Sew a narrow hem around all four sides of the shirt. Neaten neck edge and front opening with bias binding. Sew ties made from bias binding at the neck. Fit shirt on to Harry to check position of arms. Top-stitch up from bottom edge of shirt to just under the arm on each side in turn.

57

Trousers: Sew trousers together along centre front seam. Hem leg edges. Sew centre back seam and inside leg seams. Turn down waist and sew a hem deep enough to carry the elastic. Thread with elastic to fit waist. Finish off and press creases into the trousers.

Rodriguez

Height: 40cm (16in)
Plate 3; pattern graph 7

The pattern for Rodriguez is very reminiscent of the velveteen-limbed dolls with pressed faces that were produced by the British firms Chad Valley and Dean's Rag Book Company just before the Second World War. Nora Wellings also made dolls with pressed velvet or felt faces. These were her famous little velvet and cloth mascot dolls, the 'Darkies' and 'Sailor Boys'. They were very similar in style to those already mentioned, which is not so surprising when you learn that she was a designer at Chad Valley for several years before setting up her own business.

Rodriguez has a simple stockinette face with buttons for eyes. This makes him quite different from the earlier dolls, just mentioned. You might like to try and make a face mask to obtain a more faithful replica.

Materials for doll 25cm (¼yd) of 91cm (36in) wide needlecord; small piece of black velvet for shoes; small piece flesh-coloured cotton for hands; 10cm (4in) by 20cm (8in) wide stockinette; 2 black or brown domed buttons for eyes; 14g (½oz) black wool; 112g (4oz) stuffing.

Materials for clothes 25cm (10in) square wool or tweed for poncho; 30.5cm (12in) bias binding for poncho; 30.5cm (12in) square felt for sombrero; braid and cord for sombrero.

The doll *Trouser legs and shoes:* Fold shoe in half lengthways and sew around the curved edge to C. Turn right side out and stuff loosely. Position shoe at base of trouser leg (with shoe pointing upwards to waist) matching D to D and C to C. Baste in place, then fold trouser leg in half and sew across bottom, enclosing shoe, and up the side from F to E. Turn right side out and stuff to within 2.5cm (1in) of the top. Make a second shoe and trouser leg in the same way then baste both legs together as a pair. The sloped edge of the trouser leg should lie to the outside.
Body: With right sides together sew round edge leaving straight edge E through G to E open. Turn right side out and lay legs in place on front edge of body only, with right sides together. Sew legs in place (see Fig 22). Stuff body firmly, then ladder stitch bottom opening to top back of legs. Pull the shoes forwards and upwards at right angles to the trouser legs. Ladder stitch them in place.
Arms: With right sides together match A to A and B to B of a hand and arm. Sew from A to B. Fold arm in half lengthways and sew around hand and up the arm. Leave top of arm open, turn right side out. Top stitch fingers, then very carefully feed small pieces of

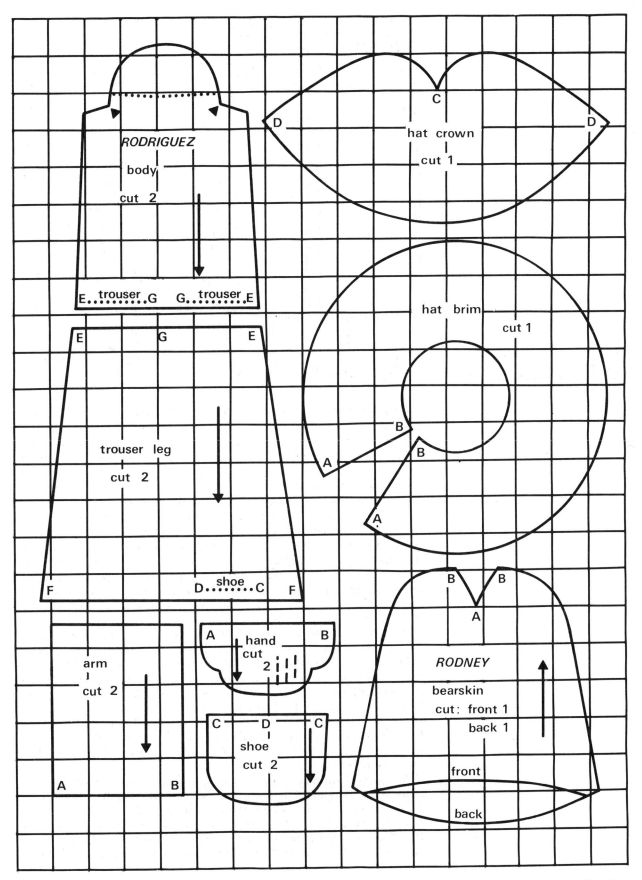

RODRIGUEZ

body

cut 2

hat crown

cut 1

E......trouser.G   G..trouser.E

E   G   E

trouser leg

cut 2

hat brim

cut 1

B

A   B

A

D......shoe....C   F

F

arm

cut 2

A   B

A   hand   B
cut
2

C   D   C

shoe

cut 2

B   B

A

RODNEY

bearskin

cut: front 1

back 1

front

back

Pattern graph 7   1 square = 2.5cm (1in)

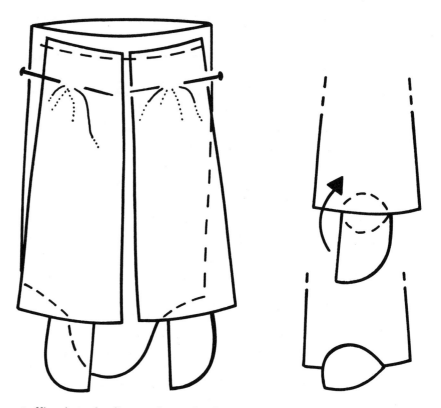

stuffing into the finger channels. Stuff palm and arm to within 2.5cm (1in) of the top. Turn seam allowance in and slip stitch edges together. Position arm across the top of the shoulder, just covering the edge and stitch securely in place. Make and attach other arm in same way, making sure that the thumbs face forwards. Hold both arms down securely by the side of the body then lift them up and down to see that they 'hinge' easily over the shoulders.

Head: Fold the stockinette in half and sew the two short ends together. This should make a 10cm (4in) deep tube. Pull down over the neck stump of the body. Arrange the seam at the back of the head (see Fig 23). With right sides together, gather head evenly on to the neck around the line marked on the pattern. Now pull head upwards and stuff firmly around the neck stump, keeping a good moulded shape. Don't stretch the stockinette. Gather up the opening on the crown and fasten off.

Hair: Cut the wool into 25cm (10in) lengths. Reserve a few strands for the moustache. Collect the hair into three equal-sized bundles and tie each one securely in the centre. Lay one bundle on top of the head from front to back and sew securely to the crown. Lay remaining two bundles across the head from side to side and again sew to the crown. Work the face before gluing the hair in position.

Facial features: Sew buttons on for eyes and pull each thread through to back of head and fasten off. The 'pull' will form eye sockets for the buttons to sink into. A few short, straight stitches make the nostrils.

Cut several strands of black wool into 6cm (2½in) lengths for the moustache. Tie the strands together in the centre with a small piece of black wool, then sew securely to the face, just below the nostrils. Pull each side of the moustache downwards and sew in place by threading a fine thread through the wool strands and pulling up slightly to give a tapered effect. Trim moustache to required shape.

60

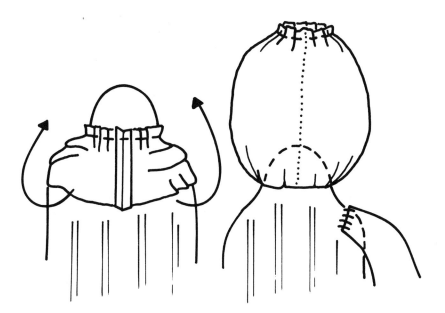

Fig 23 Rodriguez, showing construction of the stockinette head, viewed from the back

Spread a thin layer of glue on the head and press hair down firmly and evenly. Trim front hair into a fringe and neaten to a pleasing length.

The clothes

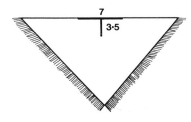

7

3·5

Fig 24 Poncho for Rodriguez, measurements of neck opening given in centimetres. (7cm = 2¾in, 3.5cm = 1½in)

Poncho: Work a row of stay stitching or zigzag on all sides, 2.5cm (1in) in from the edge. Fringe outside the stitching. Fold poncho to find centre point then cut a T-shaped neck opening as in Figure 24. Bind neck edges with bias binding, remembering to check fit over head first.

Sombrero: Overlap the edges of the brim from A to B and make a narrow, flat stab stitch seam. Fold crown and sew the side seam C to D. Sew brim and crown together with right sides facing and keep the brim seam to the centre back. Clip curve. Turn outer brim edge upwards and over by 6mm (¼in) and work tiny stab stitches through both thicknesses all round the edge, gently pulling up as you go. This will pull the brim up into the characteristic sombrero shape.

The puckering effect of gathers can be removed by ironing the edge under a damp cloth to shrink the felt. Work evenly and with patience to iron the gathers smooth and dry. Trim hat with fancy braid and stitch cord to either side. Place sombrero on head and knot the cord under the chin.

Rodney

Height: 43cm (17in)
Plate 3; pattern graph 7

Read the instructions for Rodriguez first; by making the following alterations you will then have a guardsman.

Materials for doll and clothes

Black felt for trouser legs; red felt for jacket; black felt edged with white russia braid for cuffs and collar; 3 gold beads for buttons;

black fur for bearskin; gold braid for shoulders and chin strap; white PVC or felt and buckle for belt.

The doll Make up as for Rodriguez, substituting felts where necessary. Rodney has no need for hair under the bearskin but he does have a very bushy moustache.

The clothes *Jacket:* Sew a strip of white braid down the centre front of the jacket, before joining front to back. Cut a red felt flap for the bottom of the jacket measuring 23cm (9in) by 6.5cm (2½in). Hem one long edge of this piece of felt then back stitch other long edge around the waist (of the completed doll) so that the short ends are at the centre front. Sew white braid down opening. Cover the join with a white felt or PVC belt and attach a buckle.

Decorate the jacket with gold buttons and braid epaulettes on the shoulders. Cut black felt into strips to make collar and cuffs, hem in place around wrists and neck and edge with white braid.

Bearskin: Bring B to B and make small dart from A to B on both the front and back of the bearskin. With right sides together, sew front to back leaving the base open. Turn right side out. Insert some stuffing in the bearskin then sew on to the head. Attach gold braid on either side to reach down under chin as a chin strap.

Arabella

Height: 60cm (23½in)
Plate 3; pattern graph 8

The style of this double-hinged doll is very popular with children. The easy movement of the limbs means that the doll is readily dressed and undressed. The fact that the doll can sit unsupported also increases play value. Prior to 1860, most cloth-bodied dolls were unable to sit. Some of the more shapely heads for other dolls in the book could easily be adapted to fit on to this body. It is really a very versatile pattern.

Materials for doll 40cm (16in) calico; 28cm (11in) wide by 30.5cm (12in) long striped cotton for legs; small piece dark-coloured cotton for shoes; 20cm (8in) dowel rod, 12mm (½in) diameter; 340g (12oz) stuffing; 56g (2oz) double knitting wool for hair; black felt for eyes; pink embroidery thread.

Materials for clothes 75cm (¾yd) cotton print; 35cm (14in) plain cotton for pants; narrow elastic; lace to trim; hair ribbon; snap fasteners.

The doll *Legs:* Cut two legs from the striped cotton, each measuring 14cm (5½in) by 30.5cm (12in) long. The stripes give the appearance of stockings. Now sew a pair of shoe pieces together from A to B and then open out and match against lower edge of leg. Sew in place with right sides together. Fold leg in half lengthways and sew from B, around shoe to C and up the back of the leg. Leave the top open. Clip between A and B of shoe then turn right side out. Stuff shoe and

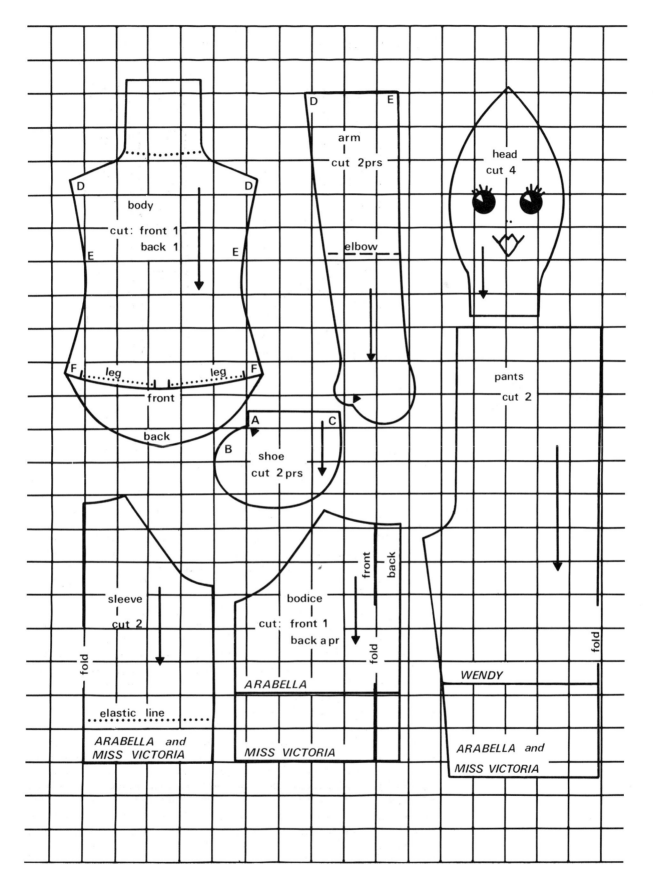

arm
cut 2prs

D   E

head
cut 4

D   D

body

cut: front 1
back 1

E   E

elbow

pants
cut 2

F   leg   leg   F

front

back

A   C

B   shoe
cut 2prs

front   back

sleeve

cut 2

bodice

cut: front 1
back a pr

fold   fold

fold

fold

WENDY

elastic line

ARABELLA

ARABELLA and
MISS VICTORIA

MISS VICTORIA

ARABELLA and
MISS VICTORIA

Pattern graph 8   1 square = 2.5cm (1in)

lower leg up to 15cm (6in) from the ankle.

Press leg flat so that the seam lies at centre back and sew across the leg with running stitches to make a knee hinge (see Fig 25). Stuff

Fig 25   Construction of legs for Arabella showing attachment of feet and the surface-stitched knee hinges

upper part of leg then make second leg in same way and baste the two legs together at the top. Put aside for the moment.

Arms: Sew arms together in pairs, leaving the top edge open. Clip thumbs and turn right side out. Stuff each arm up to the elbow line marked on pattern. Sew an elbow hinge then stuff the upper arm.

Body: Place front and back body pieces together with right sides facing. Sew from F on each side up to the neck opening and stitch arms in seams as appropriate, matching D to D and E to E. Pull on the arms to turn right side out. Lay basted legs against lower front edge and with seams of legs uppermost stitch legs to body. Stuff body firmly from the bottom. Ease the lower back edge to fit the front and ladder stitch the two together. The extra fabric at the back gives the doll a 'bottom' to sit on. Push stuffing down through open neck, check that shoulders are firm and then work the dowel rod down into the body so that only about 2.5cm (1in) is left protruding from the neck. Work stuffing around the rod then bind strong thread around top of neck to hold calico and rod together. Fasten off securely.

Head: Sew two head pieces together from crown to neck along one side only. Repeat with the remaining two head pieces then sew both completed halves of the head together from neck up to crown and down to neck again. Turn head right side out and stuff firmly. Select the smoothest side to be the front then gently ease neck of body with protruding rod into centre of head, removing stuffing if necessary. Ladder stitch the head along the line marked on pattern of body.

Facial features: Cut dark-coloured pupils for the eyes and work a small triangular highlight on each one. Hem on to face and work a few straight-stitch eyelashes. Embroider mouth and work cheeks as large, pink double crosses.

64

Hair: Cut all the wool into 46cm (18in) lengths. Sew across the end to hold together. Stitch this end to the crown then back stitch wool to head along a suitable hair-line that frames the face. Pull the free ends back up to the crown, covering all the stitching, and tie with a ribbon to make a ponytail (see Fig 26).

Fig 26   Arabella, showing construction of ponytail and the facial features

The clothes

Pants: Make the pants by following the directions given for the Shaped Crotch method in the Dressmaking section, page 30.

Dress: Cut the bodice for the dress and sleeves carefully as the same pieces of pattern are used for several other dolls. In addition you will need to cut a skirt measuring 30.5cm (12in) long by 91cm (36in) wide and a further piece measuring 7.5cm (3in) by 91cm (36in) wide. This last piece can be cut in half to make two waist ties, each 46cm (18in) long.

Start by making two darts on the waist edge of the front bodice to take up some of the fullness. Then sew sleeves to front and back bodice sections carefully so that when spread out you have a back, sleeve, front, sleeve and back piece, in correct order. Hem sleeves along the wrist edge. Work a row of elastic along the guide-line to gather up each sleeve.

Sew underarm and bodice sides in one continuous seam on each side. Make the waist ties by folding them in half widthways, right sides together, and sew one short end and the long side. Turn right side out and press. Enclose the base of the ties in the bodice side seams for preference.

Sew skirt into a tube by sewing short sides together to make a centre back seam. Leave top 5cm (2in) open. Gather up to fit waist edge of bodice. Sew skirt to bodice. Neaten back opening and hem the skirt. Gather up neck edge to fit doll. This will be approximately 18cm (7in). Keep most of the gathering on top of the sleeves, away from the front. Cut a bias strip to neaten the neck edge and decorate with lace if desired. Fit dress on to doll and determine the position of snap fasteners on the back opening. Sew at least three snaps on. Finally, press the dress before putting it on to the doll.

Some more ideas for hinged dolls

1. Use the pattern for Hilary to build up a collection of dolls representing 'Children of the World', each dressed in simplified national costumes.

2. This same pattern can be enlarged to make a very different doll. You will need to lengthen the arms. To do this, cut the arms off along the shoulder hinge line and add length to them. Stitch back on to body in the same way as the arms of Arabella.

3. Make Rodriguez in blue velvet, add a suitable hat and collar and you have a sailor. Replace the poncho with a fringed vest and you have a cowboy.

4. Arabella appears in the book again as Wendy, same doll, but very different clothes.

8 The development of jointed dolls

All manner of ingenious devices have been used to articulate dolls. These undoubtedly reflect the skill and imagination of the doll-maker, as well as current trends and the materials available at the time. The last century saw several very different kinds of jointing for cloth-bodied dolls, some of which are still popular today while others are now only of historical interest.

The early leather bodied dolls with porcelain heads were rather stiff, being stuffed with sawdust and bran. Consequently they were generally unjointed; however, it was not long before doll-makers tried to work out ways to enable them to sit. Hinges at the thighs came first followed by hinges at elbows and knees. Examples of these stitched hinges have already been given in the previous chapter.

Towards the end of the nineteenth century, elaborate gussets were being used. These worked effectively but were quite unreal to look at. Fortunately the prevailing fashions meant that they were safely hidden by clothing. This type of jointing is now only used when repairing antique dolls or as a technical exercise by a doll-maker wishing to gain experience.

Where leather bodies had china or composition lower limbs, jointing was achieved by means of rivets. This method, patented by Charles Fausel in 1896, was known as the Universal joint. Sarah Robinson also patented a method whereby the connection between limb and body was held tight by cord or thread drawn through from side to side and tied off on a button or washer. This joint was known as the *Ne Plus Ultra* and, together with the Universal joint, it replaced gussets.

At about the same time, the ball and socket joint used in hollow wood, composition, and china dolls was adapted for use in cloth bodies. The ball, made from stiffened cloth instead of wood, and two adjacent sockets were strung together with elastic. This very realistic joint closely resembled the way in which the human femur bone articulates with the pelvis. It allowed the limb to move in all directions. Elastic is still very much is use today for jointing vinyl dolls. Disc joints that allow limbs to rotate were patented at the turn of the century and are discussed in the following chapter.

Mandy, Miss Victoria and Cheko have joints that rely on sewing techniques for their effectiveness. They include examples of lap shoulders, socket shoulders, parcel hinges, flat-stitched swing hinges and, finally, gussets.

Mandy

Height: 48cm (19in)
Plates 1 and 4; pattern graphs 9 and 10

Mandy is a single-hinged doll with child-like proportions. Her head is made from three pattern pieces and is shaped to give cheeks. The

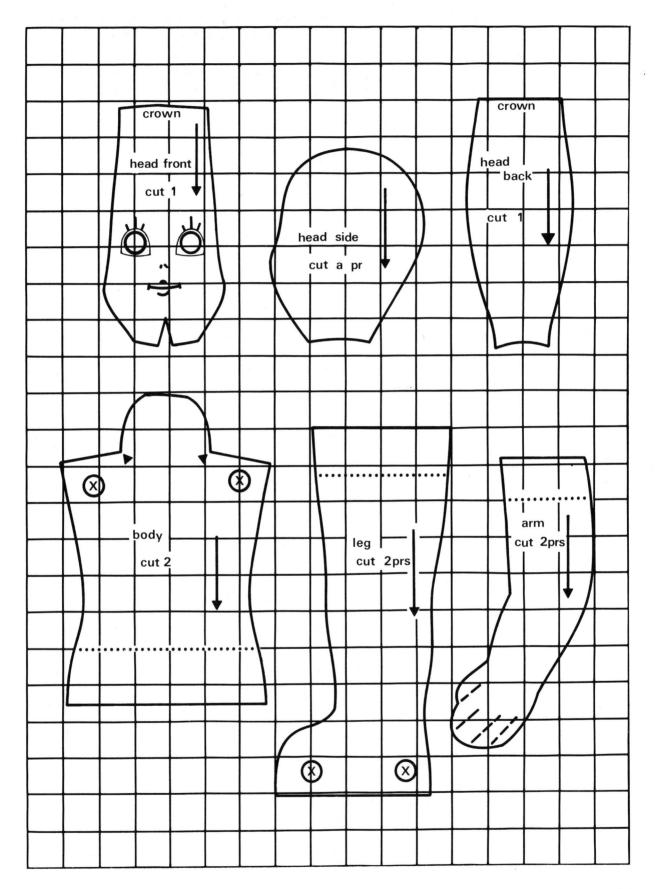

crown

head front

cut 1

head side

cut a pr

crown

head back

cut 1

body

cut 2

leg

cut 2prs

arm

cut 2prs

Pattern graph 9

1 square = 2.5cm (1in)

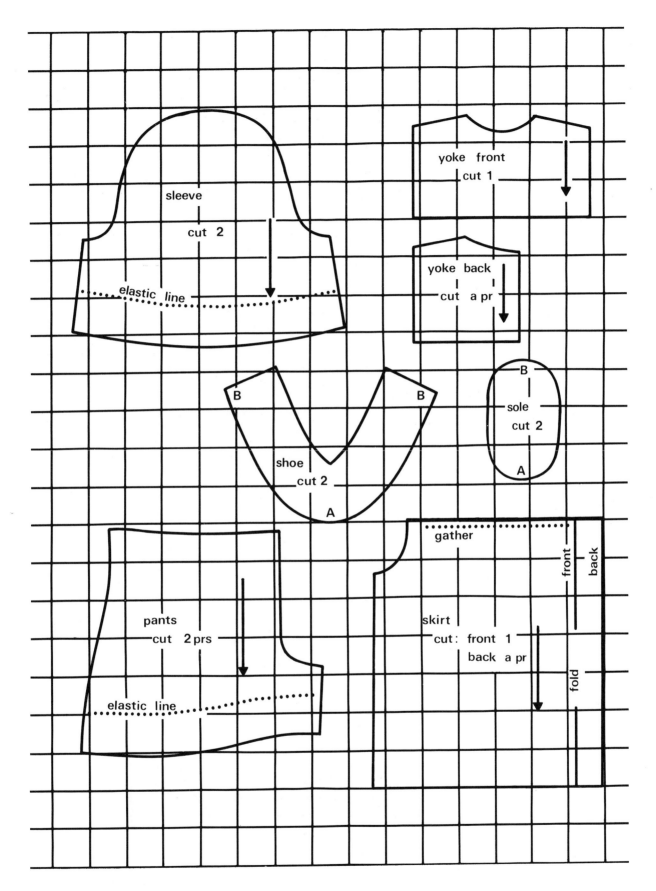

sleeve

cut 2

elastic line

yoke front
cut 1

yoke back
cut a pr

B   B

shoe
cut 2

A

B

sole
cut 2

A

gather

front

back

pants
cut 2 prs

elastic line

skirt
cut: front 1
back a pr

fold

Pattern graph 10   1 square = 2.5cm (1in)

hands have surface-stitched fingers. The joints for this doll are lap-hinged shoulders and parcel-hinged hips. Parcel hinges are not particularly attractive to look at but they do give depth to the thighs and bottom, allowing the doll to bend forwards only and to sit easily. These simply constructed hinges are similar to those used by Ada Lum when making Chinese folk dolls in her Hong Kong workshops. Her outworkers were particularly skilled seamstresses as they were able to stitch separate fingers on dolls which were often not more than 20cm (8in) tall.

Materials for doll 50cm (½yd) calico; 340g (12oz) stuffing; 28g (1oz) double knitting wool for hair; embroidery thread for facial features; colouring for cheeks.

Materials for clothes 50cm (½yd) cotton for dress; 1m (1yd) ricrac to trim dress; 3 buttons; 3 snap fasteners; 107cm (42in) elastic; 23cm (9in) square felt for shoes; 15cm (6in) by 5cm (2in) felt for shoe binding.

The doll *Body:* Sew front and back body together around all sides, leaving the straight-edged bottom open. Clip seam at neck corners and trim points off each shoulder. Now open out each shoulder in turn by pulling the front and back apart at the position marked by an X. Finger-press seams open and sew across corners at right angles to the side seam as shown in Figure 27. Turn body right side out and stuff firmly down to the line marked on the pattern. Fold both sides in towards the centre then overlap front and back edges, as you would do when closing the ends of a parcel, and slip stitch in place.
Arms: Make each arm by sewing round edge of a pair of arm pieces, leaving the top open. Clip thumb and turn arm right side out. Put a little stuffing in hand then top stitch finger divisions with tiny stab stitches. Finish stuffing arm up to line marked on pattern. Turn under the seam allowance and close arm opening by slip stitching edges together. Lay top of arm across shoulder and sew in place, making sure that the arm is able to hang down by the side of the body in a resting position.

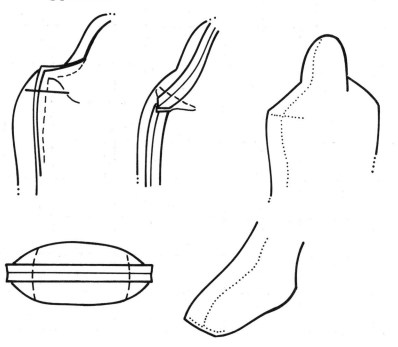

Fig 27 Mandy, showing stages in the construction of the shoulder (*above*) and the foot (*below*)

Legs: Sew a pair of leg pieces together round the edge, leaving the top open. Shape the foot, opening out the toe and heel by pulling apart at Xs marked on pattern. Sew across the seams at right angles as you did to form the shoulders (see Fig 27).

Stuff leg firmly up to line marked on pattern. Fold in sides of top opening then lap front edge over back edge and stitch in place. Make second leg in exactly the same way.

The legs are now ready to hinge to the body. Place them in position and stitch front edge of legs to front of body only, leaving the back edges unattached. This allows the body to bend forward and restricts movement backwards.

Head: Make chin dart on front of head then sew front and back head pieces together across the crown to form one long central gusset. Fit this gusset between the side head pieces, taking care to ease the fabric round the curves of the cheeks, keeping them level with each other. Sew from front neck edge to back neck edge on each side. Trim curves. Stuff head firmly, pushing stuffing well into cheeks. Push two fingers up into the centre of the head to make a cavity for the neck stump. Lower head on to neck, position centrally then ladder stitch in place, inserting any more stuffing needed to stop the head from wobbling.

Facial features: Lightly pencil in features then embroider the detail with stem stitch. The nostrils and eyelashes are small straight stitches. Finally blush the cheeks with colouring using either moistened pencil or lipstick.

Hair: Cut approximately 60 strands of wool 28cm (11in) in length. The remainder of the wool is cut into 30.5cm (12in) lengths. The bunch of shorter lengths makes the fringe. Machine or hand sew across this wool, 9cm (3½in) from the end. Lay the wool on the head with fringe frontwards and longer ends towards the back. Back stitch in place across machine line which should lie above the crown seam (see Fig 28). Sew a central parting through the remaining bunch. Position across the head, sew through the parting and also glue hair in place. Trim hair to required length when the doll is dressed and finished.

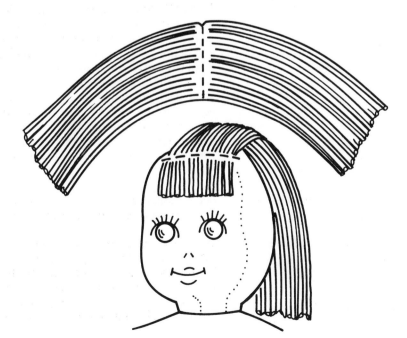

Fig 28 Mandy, showing position of wool for the hair and the facial features

The clothes

Pants: Make up by following the instructions for Shaped Crotch and Legs method given in the Dressmaking section, page 30.

Dress: Sew front and back yokes together on the shoulders. Decorate yoke with ricrac at this stage. Gather front and back top edges of skirt and sew to their respective yoke pieces. Make a narrow hem down both sides of centre back opening. Sew a narrow hem along bottom edge of each sleeve and then sew elastic along guideline, stitching it as you go. Gather the head of each sleeve so that it fits in the armhole formed by the yoke and skirt. Match centre of sleeve to shoulder seam, spread the fullness evenly and sew in place.

Sew underarm seam and side seam of dress in one continuous line. Do this on both sides. Fit dress on doll and make any adjustments necessary at the neck. Neaten neck edge with a bias strip. Hem lower edge of dress and sew on back fastenings of own choice. Decorate hem with ricrac.

Shoes: Cut felt binding for shoes in half lengthways so that you have two strips, each measuring 15cm (6in) by 2.5cm (1in). Fold a strip in half across the width and machine it to the upper edge of the shoe with the fold projecting (see Fig 29). This strengthens the shoe by protecting the felt from excessive stretching. Close back seam of shoe then insert sole matching A to A and B to B. Ease the shoe upper to fit the sole, keeping more fullness towards the toes. Turn shoe right side out and fit on doll. Make remaining shoe in same way.

Fig 29   Construction of felt shoe for Mandy

Miss Victoria

Height: 50cm (20in)
Plates 1 and 4; pattern graphs 8, 11 and 12

This doll has a hinged body that allows the limbs to bend easily. She has been designed especially for dressing up in old-fashioned clothes. Her waist is darted to cope with the bulk of skirt bands, elasticated pants and petticoat and her bottom is shaped so that she can sit easily. Her feet and head also have more shaping than any other doll encountered so far. The shoulder articulation is formed by a socket joint, while the hip and knee joints are stitched hinges. The collection of clothes for Miss Victoria includes slippers, pants, petticoat, raglan-sleeved blouse, long skirt, cape and bonnet. The patterns for the blouse and pants are included on the pattern graph for Arabella while the doll and remaining clothes each have their own pattern graph.

Materials for doll

50cm (20in) calico; 678g (1lb 8oz) stuffing; 56g (2oz) double knitting wool for hair; embroidery threads for face; colouring for cheeks.

Materials for clothes

1m (1yd) white cotton for petticoat, pants and blouse; 46cm (18in) fabric for skirt; 30.5cm (12in) velvet or needlecord for cape and bonnet; same amount of fabric for lining cape and bonnet; velvet bow for hair; satin ribbon for blouse; 3 pearl buttons; 3m (3yd) Broderie Anglaise; 2m (2yd) narrow elastic; 46cm (18in) lace to edge bonnet; 30.5cm (12in) square felt for slippers; snap fasteners; hooks and eyes.

72

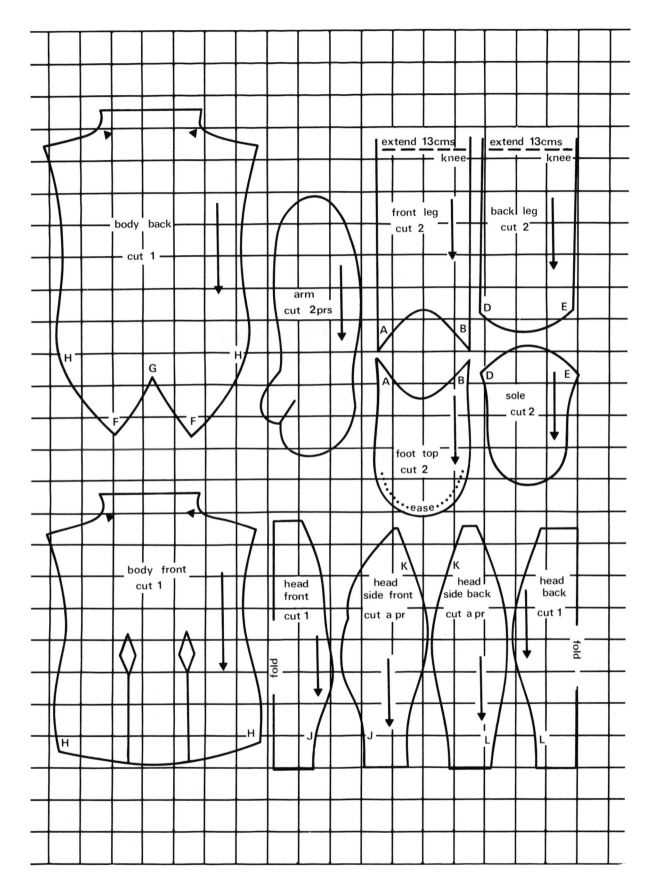

extend 13cms — knee
extend 13cms — knee

front leg
cut 2

back leg
cut 2

D   E

body back

cut 1

arm
cut 2prs

A   B

A   B   D   E

sole
cut 2

foot top
cut 2

•ease•

H   H

G

H   H

F   F

body front
cut 1

head
front

cut 1

K   K

head
side front

cut a pr

head
side back

cut a pr

head
back

cut 1

fold

fold

H   H   J   J   L   L

Pattern graph 11

1 square = 2.5cm (1in)

The doll

Legs: These need to be cut longer in order to be the correct length. The pattern pieces finish at a line level with the knee hinge, cut above this line adding another 13cm (5in). This is the upper leg section. Place each top of foot to front legs, matching A to A and B to B. Sew across from A to B. Now place soles right sides to back legs and match D to D and E to E. Sew across from D to E. Clip and trim curves

Place a front leg and back leg together, right sides facing. Pin at ankle seams and run a gathering thread around the toe, ease up until it fits the sole. Sew down side of leg, around foot and up other side of leg leaving top edge open. Turn leg right side out and stuff firmly up to the knee joint. Work a row of running stitch across the knee to form a stitched hinge. Stuff upper portion of leg to within 2.5cm (1in) of the top. Make second leg in same way. Put legs aside while you assemble the body.

Body: Start by making the two darts on the front that shape the waist then make the seating dart on the back. Fold the back to match F to F then sew from F to G. Now place both right sides of body together and sew from H up the side to the neck. Repeat on the other side leaving the neck open. Turn body right side out. Turn under seam allowance along bottom opening from H to H on both front and back bodies. Insert the top of the legs, and with toes facing forwards, position the legs evenly on either side of F which is at centre back. Machine across from H to H, hinging legs in position. Stuff body and run a gathering thread around the neck. Pull up slightly and finish off by working large stitches across the neck to hold stuffing in place.

Arms: Stitch arm pieces together in pairs leaving an opening on the shoulder. Stitch between thumb and fingers before cutting, it is easier. Turn arms right side out and stuff, close openings. To make a socket for the shoulder joint, press your finger against the side seam of the body at the very top where it turns back to the neck as the shoulder seam. By working your finger back and forth you will push up a ridge of fabric at right angles to the side seam. Place the head of the arm into the socket under the ridge just formed and sew arm to ridge as in Figure 30.

Head: Sew side fronts to front matching J to J on each side. Sew side backs to back matching L to L on each side. Now sew front and back halves of head together matching K to K on each side. Turn completed head right side out and stuff firmly. Run a gathering thread around the neck opening and pull up slightly. Position head on neck of body and ladder stitch together securely.

Facial features: Using Figure 31 as a guide, draw the face very lightly on to the head and work the embroidery as follows: small chain stitch in dark brown to make the eyebrow and to outline the eye. Use straight stitches to indicate the eyelashes and nostrils. The iris is deep turquoise satin stitch while the pupil is deep navy satin stitch. The mouth is also worked in satin stitch with the upper and lower lips being slightly parted. Blush the cheeks with colouring.

Hair: Cut all the wool into 92cm (36in) lengths. Sew a central parting 14cm (5½in) wide then sew the wool on to the head by back stitching through the centre parting. Pull wool down on either side of face and back towards where the ears would be and sew just above the nape of the neck (see Fig 32). Now pull all the wool back up to the crown and stitch down to form a ponytail. There will be too much bulk in the wool but by working two small plaits you can reduce this bulk. These plaits are formed from the ponytail strands. Work one on each side and then pull down under the unplaited strands and

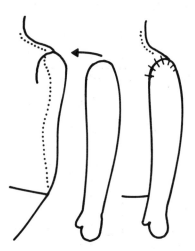

Fig 30   Miss Victoria, showing construction of socket hinge for the shoulder

Fig 31   Facial features for Miss Victoria

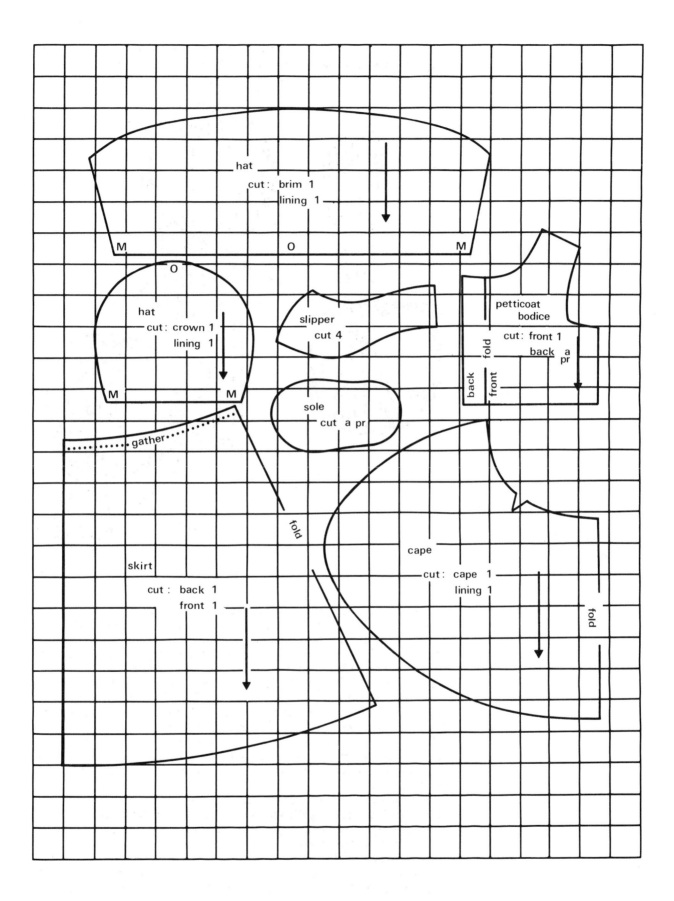

hat

cut : brim 1
lining 1

M   O   M

O

hat

cut : crown 1
lining 1

M   M

gather

slipper
cut 4

sole
cut a pr

petticoat
bodice

cut : front 1
back a pr

fold

back front

fold

skirt

cut : back 1
front 1

cape

cut : cape 1
lining 1

fold

Pattern graph 12   1 square = 2.5cm (1in)

fasten off. Cover the ends with the ponytail and hold the ponytail in place by sewing a flat velvet bow over the join (see Fig 32).

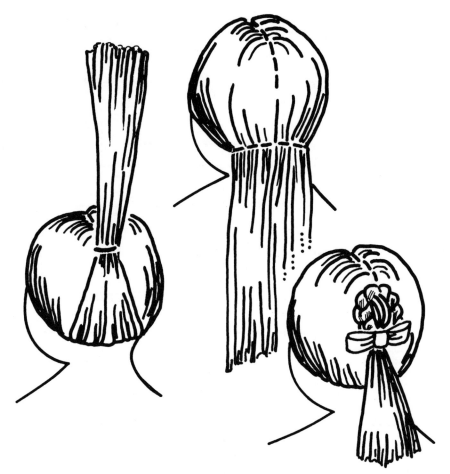

Fig 32   Stages in the construction of the ponytail for Miss Victoria

The clothes   *Pants:*   Make the pants by following the directions given for the Shaped Crotch method in the Dressmaking section, page 30. Decorate the ankle edges with lace.

Petticoat: Cut a skirt for the petticoat measuring 25cm (10in) long by 92cm (36in) wide. Sew bodice backs to front on the shoulders and side seams. Gather up skirt to fit waist edge then sew to bodice. Neaten neck and armholes with bias binding. Fold over back edges and hem. Sew on hooks and eyes for fasteners at neck and waist. Hem petticoat and edge with Broderie Anglaise.

Blouse: The pattern for the blouse is also used to make the bodice for the dress worn by Arabella. The blouse, however, is cut longer so that it can tuck safely into the skirt. Also the darts of the dress are omitted on the blouse.

Sew sleeves between front and back pieces. Decorate front of blouse with a piece of gathered lace edged on to satin ribbon. Gather up neck edge to fit doll. Remember that Miss Victoria and Arabella have different-sized necks.

Finish constructing blouse by following instructions given for Arabella, hemming the waist edge to finish and decorating the wrist edges with Broderie Anglaise. Sew the pearl buttons on the front.

76

Skirt: Cut a waistband for the skirt measuring 35cm (14in) by 7.5cm (3in). Sew both side seams of the skirt, leaving an opening at the waist edge on one side. Gather up waist of skirt to fit doll and then sew on waistband. Close waist opening with hook and eye. Hem skirt edge.

Cape: Sew the small shoulder dart on each side of the cape and the cape lining. Place right sides together of the cape and lining and sew all around the edge leaving only the neck edge open. Clip and trim curve. Turn cape right side out and press. Cut a bias strip of velvet or needlecord to neaten the neck edge. Sew on a hook and eye at the front to fasten the cape.

Bonnet: Sew the curved edge of the crown to the straight edge of the brim matching M to M at both ends and O to O in the centre. Make the lining in the same way. Place right sides together of bonnet and lining and sew all around the edge of the brim leaving the straight edge of the crown open. Trim and clip curve. Turn right side out and press. Slip stitch opening closed. Gather a length of lace and use to decorate the front edge of the bonnet. Hem it to the lining so that it projects forwards under the brim.

Slippers: Sew both slipper sides together along a narrow centre front seam. Cut a strip of felt 20cm (8in) by 2.5cm (1in). Fold this in half, widthways and baste long edges together. Ease upper edge of slipper to fit the felt strip and then sew them together as for Mandy. Sew centre back seam, then insert sole and sew in place, easing toe in to fit sole. Make second slipper in same way.

Cheko the Clown

Height: 61cm (24in)
Plate 4; pattern graph 13

Cheko is the only doll in the book with gusset joints. These are at the knees and elbows where they prevent the legs and arms from bending backwards or forwards in the wrong direction. The joints are hidden by the costume which is stitched permanently on to the body. In addition he has hinged shoulders, hips and waist which allow for even more mobility. With a few simple alterations and additions this doll could easily become a string puppet character. The wrist and ankles would need to be articulated and the head would need the dowel rod and neck stuffing removed. In addition, weights would have to be placed in the feet and hands and on the bottom. You will notice that the hands have three fingers and a thumb which again is quite usual for puppets.

This is a difficult pattern to make up successfully but as long as you have made several other styles first and proceed carefully with this one you should have no great problems.

Materials for doll
50cm (½yd) calico; 25cm (¼yd) stockinette or similar stretch fabric for head and hands; 56g (2oz) double knitting wool for hair; 556g (1lb 4oz) stuffing; small pieces of white, red, black and green felt for face, a pair of 15mm shallow, domed black buttons for the eyes; cheek colouring; 13cm (5in) dowel rod, 12mm (½in) diameter.

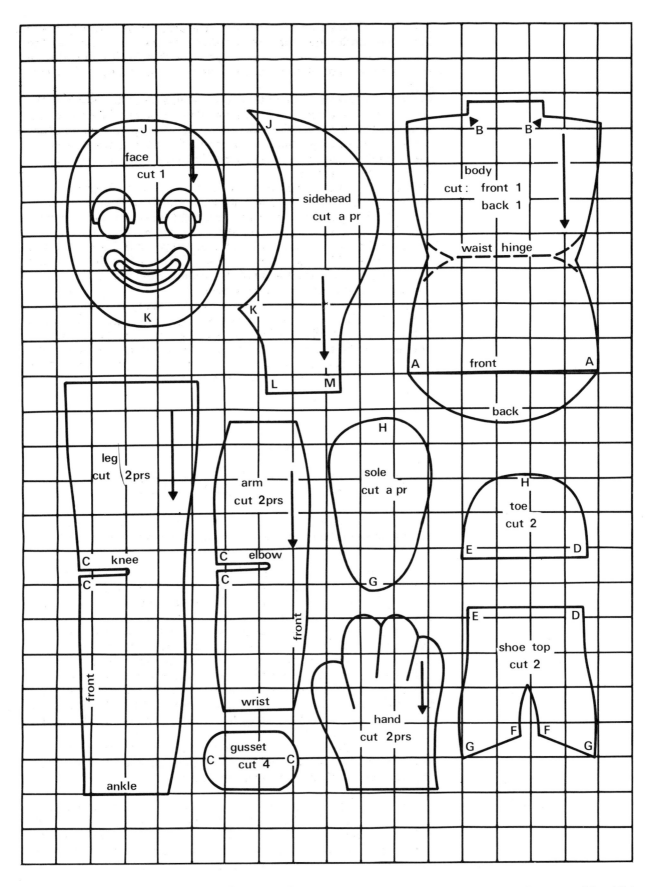

face
cut 1

J

K

sidehead
cut a pr

J

K

L M

body
cut : front 1
      back 1

B B

waist hinge

A front A

back

leg
cut 2prs

arm
cut 2prs

sole
cut a pr

H

G

toe
cut 2

H

E D

C knee

C

C elbow

C

front

H

shoe top
cut 2

E D

front

wrist

hand
cut 2prs

F F

G G

C gusset
cut 4 C

ankle

Pattern graph 13

1 square = 2.5cm (1in)

Materials for clothes   1m (1yd) gingham; plain-coloured cotton to edge frills, optional; 23cm (9in) square felt for shoes; 23cm (9in) square contrasting coloured felt for shoes.

The doll   *Body:* Cut the body and limbs from calico. Sew front and back body pieces together, up each side from A, across shoulders to B. This leaves both the neck and the bottom open. Top stitch the waist hinge by following the guide-line marked on the pattern. Stuff upper portion of body through the neck, leave open. Stuff lower portion of body from lower edge then ease curved back to fit front edge and ladder stitch the two together.

Arms: Sew a pair of arm pieces together along the back seam from shoulder to wrist, breaking the stitching at the elbow slit. Insert a gusset at the elbow, matching C to C on top and bottom of slit at the seam. Baste in position before sewing. Sew arm pieces together along the front seam. Turn right side out and stuff carefully from both open ends. Do not push too much stuffing in front of the elbow as you might distort the joint and spoil the movement. Turn seam allowance of shoulder opening in and slip stitch edges together. Sew arm in position over the shoulder as a lap joint. Make other arm in same way.

Hands: Draw outline of hand on to a square of double thickness stockinette. Pin corners of square to hold both pieces together then sew outline of hand inside the pencil line. Stitch down between each finger and square off the base rather than sewing to a point. Leave wrist edge open. Cut away excess fabric round hand and slash between the fingers. Turn right side out and stuff, being careful not to distort the shape of the hand by stretching the stockinette. Sew the hand on to the wrist edge of an arm, making sure that the thumb faces forward when the arm hangs at rest. Make the other hand.

Legs: These are made in the same way as the arms, inserting gussets at the knee slits. Turn legs right side out and stuff carefully from both ends. Turn in the seam allowance at the top of the legs and press them flat so that the two seams lie over each other at centre back and centre front. Sew legs in position to lower front edge of the body. The shoes take the place of feet and are sewn directly on to the ankle. The point to watch is that the gusset lies to the front of the leg and to the back of the arm.

Shoes: Seam toe to top shoe matching D to D and E to E. Close back ankle seam from F to G. Insert sole matching G to G and H to H then sew in place. Turn shoe right side out, stuff and ladder stitch securely to the base of the leg. Make second shoe in the same way.

Head: Cut the face and side heads from stockinette. Seam the two side heads together from J to M and the under chin seam from K to L. Now run an easing thread round the face, pulling up evenly so that it can be positioned J to J and K to K. Arrange most of the fullness on the lower half of the face. Turn head right side out and stuff. Great care must be taken when stuffing the stockinette as it easily stretches into unwanted ugly shapes. Start by pushing the stuffing forwards to mould out the face, keep the head rounded and as you proceed, insert the dowel rod. Finish stuffing the neck and close around the dowel leaving approximately 4cm (1½in) protruding. Push dowel into neck opening of body and ladder stitch head and body together securely.

Hair: Wind the wool on to the widest setting of the Quadframe and make rows of curls. Alternatively turn wool into a suitable length fringe. Back stitch hair on to head from side to side leaving the top bald.

Facial features: Cut a circle of felt with a 5cm (2in) diameter. Gather up the edge and insert a knobble of stuffing before fastening off. Sew nose in position on face. Sew red felt to white felt for mouth then stitch in place. The eyes are made by sewing the black buttons to black felt then hemming the units to larger circles of white felt. Hem the green eye backings to the face and then sew eye units on to the green felt (see Fig 33). Blush the cheeks gently with lipstick or rouge.

The clothes

Fig 33   Position of facial features for Cheko the Clown

Costume: These instructions are for a costume that is stitched on to the doll. Fold the fabric in half twice, first widthwise and then lengthwise. Following Figure 34, cut out the costume. Figure 35 shows the unfolded fabric. Cut a T for the neck and front opening. Lay the doll flat on the costume and then slash the material between the legs. Hem wrist edges. Sew underarm and side seam continuously. Hem ankle edge then sew inside leg seam up to the crotch and down the other side.

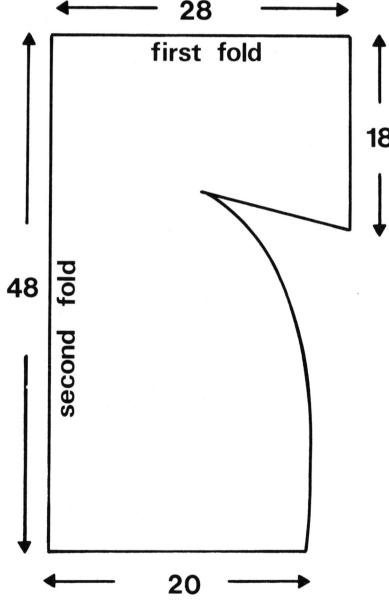

Fig 34   Costume for Cheko with measurements given in centimetres. (18cm = 7in, 20cm = 8in, 28cm = 11in, 48cm = 19in)

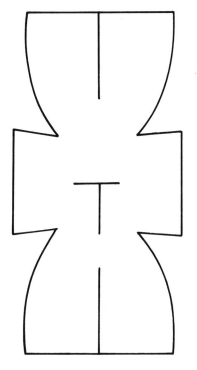

Turn costume right side out and fit it on to the doll. Turn the neck edge under and slip stitch to the body. Close front opening. Gather wrists and ankles on to the respective limbs.

From the remaining gingham, cut strips to make frills for the neck and wrists. These frills are more effective if a bold-coloured fabric is used to edge them.

Some more ideas for jointed dolls

1. Dress Mandy as a tomboy by using the clothes designed for Norman.
2. Insert a disc joint in the neck of Miss Victoria.
3. Ignore the waist hinge when making Cheko and replace the gusset hinges with stitched swing hinges. You will still have a double hinged doll but it will be less articulated.
4. Make stilts for Cheko by following Figure 36. If the stilts were made even longer, Cheko could perform with string puppets on a stage.

Fig 35   Costume for Cheko shown opened out and position of T slash for neck opening

Fig 36   Cheko mounted on lengths of dowelling. His hands and feet are tied on to the dowelling with tape while the head is supported by strong millinery elastic threaded through small holes in the rods

9 Pivot-jointed dolls

These dolls have limbs that rotate around an axis. Thus the arms are pivoted to move freely parallel with, but clear of, the body, while the legs are set inside the body outline with the hip joints placed on a diagonal. If the legs were left to turn outside the body, like the arms, then the upper and lower limbs could not move freely as they would tend to become caught up with each other. The body would also appear distorted with bulging hips and widely spaced legs. Diagonal hip joints allow the legs to spread when the doll sits down, and, in some instances, to stand unaided. Standing is not easy for cloth dolls. They must be designed with the centre of gravity passing through flat feet and are more successful if the lower legs are filled with compacted sawdust or a mixture of sand and glue.

There are two popular ways of using pivot joints. The first, thought to have originated in China, uses strong cord, elastic or wire to join the limbs together through the body. The second, more modern, method uses two discs and a cotter pin and it is this form that is now widely used to joint soft dolls. Norman is an example of the former while Annette illustrates the latter. Gerry, the first doll in this chapter, has rather unusual joints formed by snap fasteners. Although these do not allow the limbs to pivot quite so freely as the other joints, the doll can nonetheless be placed in a variety of different poses.

Gerry

Length: 19cm (7½in)
Plate 5; pattern graph 14

Baby dolls as we know them, with bent limbs, feet facing inwards, shortened necks and short hair, are a development of the late nineteenth and early twentieth centuries. Prior to this time, the term 'baby' generally referred to all dolls, irrespective of their proportions and whether they were dressed as babies or not.

Dolls modelled from real life babies were the most popular and proved best-sellers on both sides of the Atlantic. Although the majority were made of bisque, two made from chemically treated fabric are worthy of special mention. In the United States, Martha Chase designed a life-sized stockinette baby doll for hospitals. This washable doll was used for training nurses in how to care for a baby. Meanwhile in Germany, Kathe Kruse was designing sand-weighted baby dolls, using her own children as models. The muslin heads of her dolls were stiffened, painted and then sprayed with fixative so that they were washable.

Gerry is a small jointed felt baby. The joints are snap fasteners

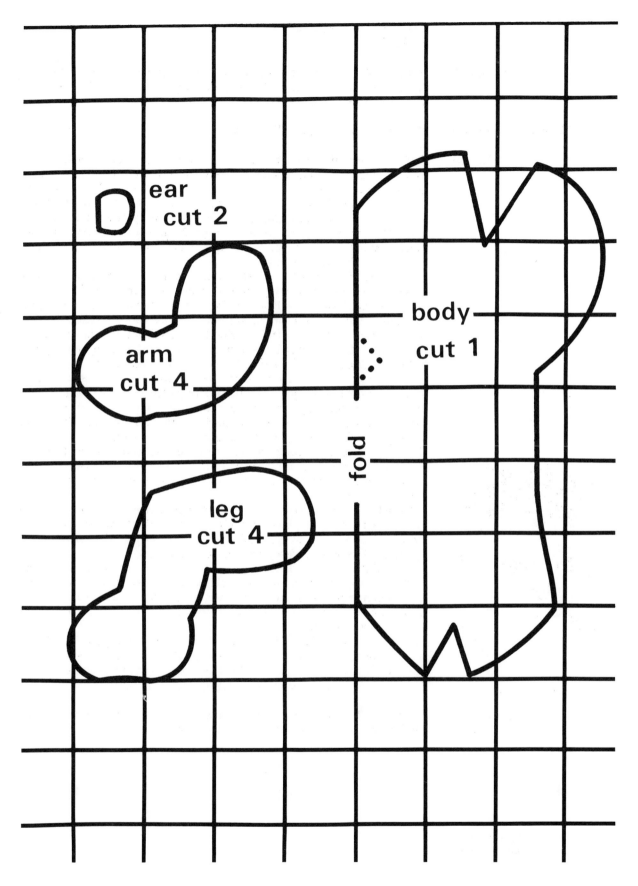

ear
cut 2

body
cut 1

arm
cut 4

fold

leg
cut 4

Pattern graph 14

1 square = 2.5cm (1in)

which gives reasonable movement for such a small doll. He is not washable.

Materials for doll 30.5cm (12in) square of flesh-coloured felt; four No 7 snap fasteners; 228cm (8ft) wool for hair; 56g (2oz) stuffing; brown-, black-, red- and blue-coloured pencils for face.

Materials for clothes 23cm (9in) square of muslin; small safety pin.

The doll *Body:* Remember that felt only requires a 3mm seam allowance. Make the darts on each side of the head and the bottom then sew along the dotted line marked on the folded edge of the pattern to shape the chin. Snip the chin shaping. Bring edges of head and body together and sew from forehead around to the middle of the centre back. Sew from base of stomach around the curved bottom to the back, leaving an opening. Turn right side out and stuff, carefully bulking out the shaping of the head.

The neck is formed by first working a row of running stitches between the head and body. Secure a double thread at the back of the neck and then take a few running stitches towards the front, pull up, and secure; work forward again with a few more stitches and so on until the neck is encircled. Further definition can be given by winding a strong thread around the neck and pulling up tightly before tying off. Darn in ends of thread before cutting.

Arms and legs: You will find these easier to do if you first cut them to a rough outline shape, sew, then trim to the pattern outline. Sew around the outer edge of each arm and leg leaving a small opening towards either the shoulder or thigh on the under side. Turn the limbs right side out and stuff, taking care not to stretch the felt at this stage. Close openings and sew respective half of snap fastener on inside head of each limb. Hold each limb in turn against the body to locate and mark position of second half of the snap fastener before sewing in place.

Glue two layers of felt together and when perfectly dry cut out the ears. Sew each ear in place by taking stitches right through the head from side to side. A slight pull on the stitches will flatten the ears against the head and also give additional shaping.

Hair: Cut wool into 12.5cm (5in) lengths and tie securely in the middle. Place wig on top of head and hold temporarily in place with a glass-headed pin. Tease out the yarn then glue to head so that side darts and seam on the forehead are covered. Trim ends to desired length. Remove the pin.

Facial features: Mark in features with coloured pencils. Use a warm brown rather than black to outline the eyes, the eyebrows and nostrils. Draw the mouth and blush the cheeks with the same colour. Colour each iris blue and the pupil black (see Fig 37).

Fig 37   Facial features for Gerry

The clothes *Nappy:* Make a hem round the edge of the muslin square then fit on doll and pin in place with a small safety pin.

Plate 5   PIVOT-JOINTED DOLLS
Left to right Gerry (undressed and dressed), Norman, Annette

Norman

Height: 50cm (20in)
Plates 1 and 5; pattern graph 15

Norman is essentially the same doll as Mandy, but the pattern has been adapted so that the limbs pivot on a wire. The head is disc-jointed to the body. This was the same method used by Chad Valley and some other manufacturers in Britain at the beginning of the twentieth century before they changed to using all disc joints. The trousers and shirt are designed slightly on the loose side so that they do not restrict the movement of the limbs.

Materials for doll 50cm (20in) calico; one, 45mm (1¾in) joint for neck; 30.5cm (12in) of 1.60mm wire; four, 5mm (³⁄₁₆in) metal washers; 340g (12oz) stuffing; 28g (1oz) double knitting wool for hair; embroidery thread for facial features.

Materials for clothes 30.5cm (12in) denim, 2 buttons and 1 hook for trousers; 20cm (8in) small check, 3 buttons and interfacing for shirt; 23cm (9in) square bright cotton for neckchief; black felt for shoes as given for Mandy, page 70.

The doll *Body:* Sew the two front bodies together down the centre front seam and the two back bodies together down the centre back seam. Leave an opening in the back seam for turning, jointing and stuffing. Sew front and back bodies together down both side seams. Cut a circle of calico to fit the neck opening and sew in place. This will measure approximately 5cm (2in) in diameter. Turn body right side out and leave for the moment.
Head: Make head by following pattern and instructions for Mandy. Turn right side out and stuff very firmly down to the neck opening. Using a pair of snipe-nosed pliers, remove the various parts of the disc joint until you have one disc and one washer only left on the split cotter pin. Cut two circles of calico, each with a diameter of 6cm (2½in), and push the ends of the cotter pin through the centre of both circles. Gather up the edges of the calico circles around the disc and fasten off. Turn under seam allowance on neck edge of head and insert the covered disc with the cotter pins protruding outwards. Ladder stitch the disc to the head, inserting more stuffing if needed as you close the opening.
   Make a hole in the centre of the calico circle which is in the neck of the body. Push cotter pins through the opening and thread on the disc and washer in that order. Slightly part the halves of the cotter pin and then pull tightly on one pin as you bend it over with snipe-nosed pliers to loop down and lock against the disc, forming one side of a crown joint (see Fig 38). Bend the remaining pin down in the same way to complete the joint. Stuff body really firmly but do not close until all the pivot joints have been made.
Legs: Make the legs by following the directions for Mandy, page 71. Continue the seam around the curved hip edge and leave an opening at the top back edge for turning. Make foot as directed then turn leg right side out, stuff firmly and close opening. Complete the second leg in the same way.
Arms: Make the arms by following the directions for Mandy, page 70. Continue the seam around the curved shoulder leaving an

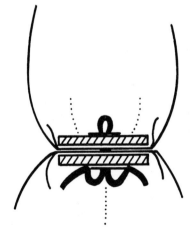

Fig 38 Norman, showing the disc joint between head and body

Plate 6 USEFUL DOLLS
Back row, left to right Wee Willie Winkie, Sleepy Sue, Wendy;
Centre Julia, Jane;
Front row FLAT DOLLS
Lavender Lil, Emily

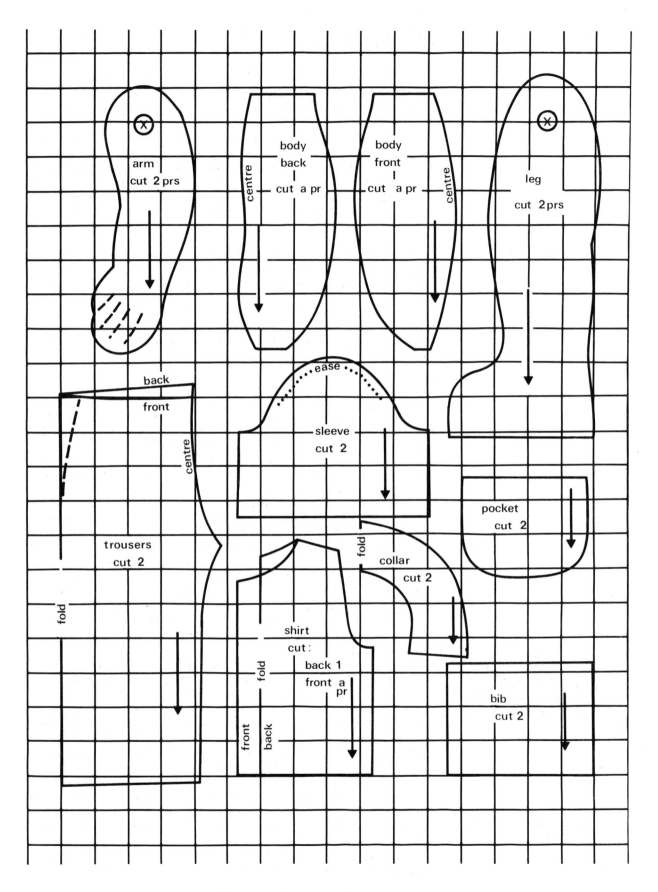

arm
cut 2 prs

body
back
centre
cut a pr

body
front
cut a pr
centre

leg
cut 2 prs

back
front
centre

ease
sleeve
cut 2

fold

pocket
cut 2

trousers
cut 2

fold

collar
cut 2

shirt
cut :
back 1
front a
pr

front
back

bib
cut 2

fold

front
fold
back

Pattern graph 15   1 square = 2.5cm (1in)

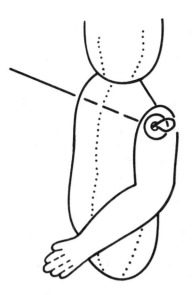

Fig 39 Norman, showing how the wire is positioned from an arm through the body and locked against a washer to make a pivot joint

Fig 40 Facial features for Norman

The clothes

opening on the back edge for turning and stuffing. Complete both arms so that they are stuffed and ready for jointing.

Making the pivot joints: Push a steel knitting needle through the arm at the spot marked by an X. Then, with the arm still on the needle, work the needle through the body at the shoulder level and out the other side. Thread on the second arm by passing the needle through the spot marked by an X. Take a 15cm (6in) length of wire and form a small loop at one end. Thread on a metal washer and push up against the loop. Remove an arm from the needle and push the sharp end of the wire through the channel formed by the needle. Remove body from needle and push wire through and finally thread on the last arm and a washer. Pull up tightly on the wire, cut off the excess wire and turn the end into a loop to lock against the washer (see Fig 39). Knock the loops over with a hammer so that they lie flat against the washers.

Pivot the legs on to the body in exactly the same way. By now the stuffing in the body will need rearranging and maybe more added. When satisfied with the shape, close the opening.

Facial features: These are worked in embroidery threads. Chain stitch is used to outline the eye while stem stitch is used to work the iris, pupil and mouth. The freckles are scattered french knots. Figure 40 shows the arrangement of the features.

Hair: Cut all the wool into 30.5cm (12in) lengths. Sew a 7.5cm (3in) wide side parting, 10cm (4in) in from the end. Attach the hair to the head by back stitching through the parting. Spread a layer of glue under the wool and press down. When the glue is completely dry and the doll is finished, layer cut the hair so that it looks like a young lad's.

Shirt: Sew fronts of shirt to the back on the shoulder seams. Slightly ease the head of each sleeve with a row of gathering stitch and fit into armhole edge. Sew in place. Hem wrist edges of sleeves. Join each underarm and side of shirt in one continuous seam. Hem the front openings and waist edge of shirt. Sew the two collar pieces together along both straight edges and the outer curved edge, using a piece of interfacing to strengthen if necessary. Trim seams of collar, turn right side out and press edges.

Select one side to be the upper collar. Check the neck edge of the shirt against the doll for size before attaching the collar. Sew right side of upper collar to wrong side of shirt. Clip seam and trim. Turn shirt over and with right side of shirt facing, turn under the seam allowance of lower collar and pin in place (see Fig 41). Sew across

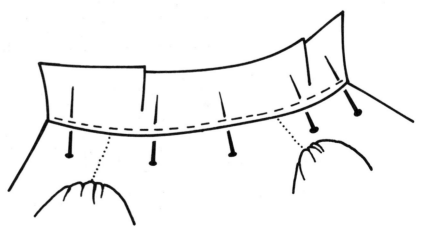

Fig 41 Norman showing construction of shirt collar

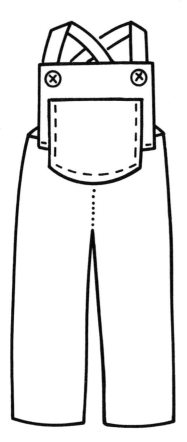

Fig 42   Trousers for Norman

from side to side. This is an open-neck shirt so sew on buttons and work buttonholes on the lower part only.

Neckerchief: Hem all sides of neckerchief and fold in half diagonally. Knot around neck, leaving enough space for the disc joint to turn.

Trousers: With right sides facing, join both trouser pieces down the centre front seam. Trim seam. Open out trousers and sew the curved hip darts on each side. Hem lower leg edges. Sew centre back seam but leave the top waist edge open for about 6cm (2½in). Sew inside leg seams from ankle up to crotch on both sides. Hem waist edge and centre back opening. Sew hook and eye on at waist to close trousers. Make the bib by sewing both pieces together with right sides facing. Leave a small opening for turning. Make the pocket in the same way. Turn both right side out, close the openings and press.

Position bib on centre front of trousers and top-sew both together along the waistline. Now place pocket on bib so that it covers most of the waistline join and sew by top stitching around the curved edge of the pocket (see Fig 42). Cut two straps for the trousers, each measuring 20cm (8in) by 5cm (2in). Sew long edges of each strap together. Turn right side out, neaten the ends and press. Sew each strap on to back waist edge of trousers and attach to top corners of bib with snap fasteners. Sew buttons on top corners of bib to hide the snap fasteners.

Shoes: Make these by following the directions given for Mandy's shoes, page 72.

Annette

Height: 33cm (13in)
Plate 5; pattern graph 16

This little dancer has disc-jointed arms and legs and a swivel-jointed neck. The swivel joint is made by first sewing a large flat button on to the base of the neck to form a flange. This flange and part of the neck are then secured in the body by closing the shoulder seam around the neck to form a collar, thus leaving the head free to rotate. Other types of flanges have included thick cord wound around the neck and ridges formed from various compositions.

Materials for doll   30.5cm (12in) calico; 15cm (6in) by 45cm (18in) dacron or courtelle wadding; 23cm (9in) flesh-coloured stockinette; 170g (6oz) stuffing; 14g (½oz) 4 ply wool for hair; two 32mm (1¼in) joints for legs; two 25mm (1in) joints for arms; 10cm (4in) of 13mm (½in) diameter dowel rod; 32mm (1¼in) button for neck swivel; 15mm (½in) round bead for nose; card for soles; coloured pencils for face; colouring for cheeks; black fibre-tip pen.

Materials for clothes   23cm (9in) of 130cm (52in) wide white net; 30.5cm (12in) swansdown; 25cm (10in) floral braid; 23cm (9in) pink taffeta or satin; hooks and eyes; narrow pink ribbon for ballet shoes.

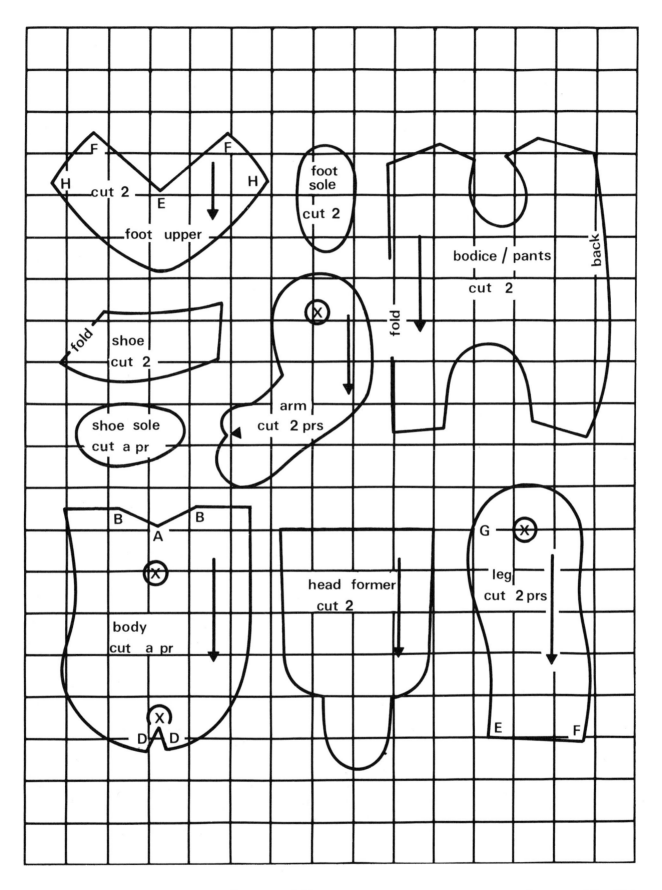

F

F

H

cut 2

H

E

foot upper

foot
sole
cut 2

bodice / pants

back

cut 2

fold

fold

shoe
cut 2

ⓧ

shoe sole
cut a pr

arm
cut 2 prs

B

B

A

ⓧ

ⓧ

G

ⓧ

body
cut a pr

head former
cut 2

leg
cut 2 prs

ⓧ

E

F

D

D

Pattern graph 16

1 square = 2.5cm (1in)

The doll

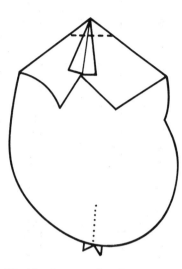

Fig 43   Annette, showing construction of a shoulder seam across the shoulder dart

Body: Working on wrong side of each body piece in turn, make the hip and shoulder darts. Fold to bring D to D then sew from D to X. This X also marks the position of the leg joint. Then fold to bring B to B and sew from A to B. Lay body on table with right side facing and fold down the shoulder dart as in Figure 43. Sew across the dart at right angles to make a seam 3cm (1¼in) long. Sew body pieces together leaving the neck end open and a part of the centre back seam. Turn right side out and leave empty for jointing.

Arms: Sew a pair of arm pieces together leaving the shoulder curve open. Turn right side out and stuff. Prepare a disc joint by removing a washer and a disc. Put the rest of the joint, which will be a pin with washer and disc, inside the arm and push the pin through the calico at the point marked by an X on the pattern. Ladder stitch the edges of the shoulder together, inserting more stuffing as you close the seam. Make the second arm in the same way being very careful to joint the arm on the correct side so that you have a pair.

Legs: Take a pair of leg pieces and sew the front leg seam from G to E. Sew foot upper to leg matching E to E and F to F on each side. Sew back seam of leg from a point level with G down to H. Turn leg right side out. Cut soles from stiff card and also cut calico soles that are larger than the pattern piece given. Lay card sole on calico and sew a gathering thread around the edge of the calico. Pull up on thread until calico rolls over edge of card. Fasten off. Turn under seam allowance at lower edge of foot upper, insert covered sole and sew the two together. Stuff leg and insert joint at hip. Close off and make second leg in same way. Again, be careful not to make two left legs or two right ones.

Taking each limb in turn, push the pin through the side of the body at the position marked by X. Thread on to the pin a disc and a washer in that order. Using snipe-nosed pliers, open out the halves of the pin and, taking each half in turn, bend back tightly against the disc to lock into a jointing position. Stuff body firmly and then close the opening in the centre back seam. Leave the top neck end open.

Head: The head for this doll is built around a former. Layers of stuffing provide chin, cheeks and forehead while stitches produce eye sockets and a bead is used to make the nose. The head is then covered with stockinette that is glued to the modelling.

Start by making the head-former. Sew both pieces together round all sides leaving top straight edge open. Turn right side out. Insert dowel rod, pushing it well down into the neck. Pack stuffing evenly around the rod and continue until the former is full. Close top opening. Cut wadding into two 15cm (6in) squares, then fold each one as indicated in Figure 44 enclosing a small amount of extra stuffing in the centre. Lay one band around the former so that the bulk forms the chin. Catch ends of band down at back of head. Lay second band across top of former to make the forehead, again catch ends down at back. Figure 44 is a side view of the head at this stage showing how the bands make the fullness of the face with a prominent chin. Sew the bead on to the lower band in a position level with the nose. Now take the remaining piece of wadding and place it diagonally across the front of the head and neck. Turn the corners down on to the back of the head and stitch in place. The neck is a little tricky to do neatly but if you work slowly and catch it down from side to side under the chin the end result will look smooth.

The head can now be covered with the first layer of stockinette. Cut a 20cm (8in) square of stockinette and place it diagonally across the head as in Figure 45. Use pins to hold it in place, stretching it across the face and tightly under the chin. Gather up the edges on

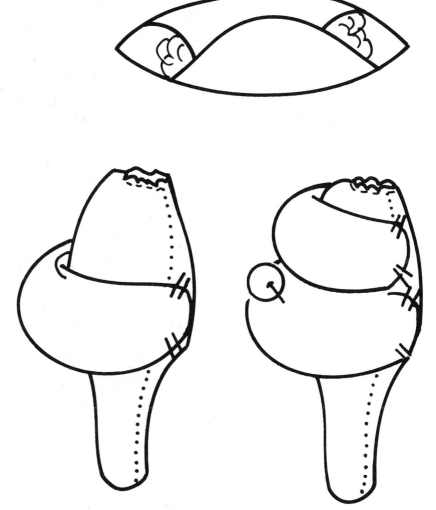

Fig 44   Annette, showing wadding folded into bands and stitched on to the head-former to make the chin and forehead. A bead is sewn on to lower band to make nose

the back of the head and turn the ends in on the back of the neck to make a neat seam (see Fig 45). Sew the button on to the base of the neck.

Make the eye sockets by working two straight stitches through the head. As you tie them off at the back, pull up tightly to sink the stitches on the front of the face. Cut another 20cm (8in) square of

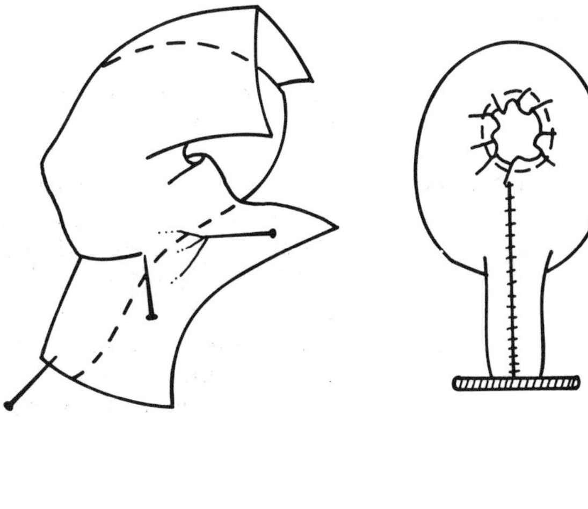

Fig 45   Head for Annette showing first layer of stockinette pulled across face and stitched down at the back. A button is sewn on to the end of the neck

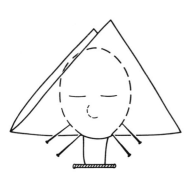

Fig 46 Annette, showing position of second layer of stockinette placed across face

stockinette and fold it in half diagonally. Place the fold under the chin and hold in place with pins (see Fig 47). Turn back the flaps, away from the face, and spread a thin layer of Copydex or similar glue over the eyes, nose and cheeks. Wait until glue becomes tacky then press under layer of stockinette on to face, removing any crinkles. Stitch the ends of this layer down on back of head.

When the face is quite dry, spread on another layer of glue and press down top layer of stockinette. Finish in same way. Hem fold of stockinette under the chin. The head is now ready to attach to the body. Push your fingers through the shoulder opening on the top of the body, press the stuffing down and then insert the button end of the neck. Put more stuffing on top of the button and close shoulder seams on either side of the neck so that the button is enclosed in the body. Do not stitch the neck fabric to the shoulder seams as this would prevent the head from rotating.

Hair: Wind wool into a skein that is 33cm (13in) long. Do not cut the loops at the ends. Sew a side parting, 12.5cm (5in) from the end and make the parting at least 9cm (3½in) wide. Sew wool on to head by back stitching through the parting. Collect loops down at back of head, stitching the shortest ones down first and winding the longer looped ends into a bun at the nape of the neck. Hide the ends with a bow if necessary (see Fig 47).

Facial features: The face is drawn on to the doll with moistened coloured pencils. Outline the eyes with a fine point fibre-tip pen after

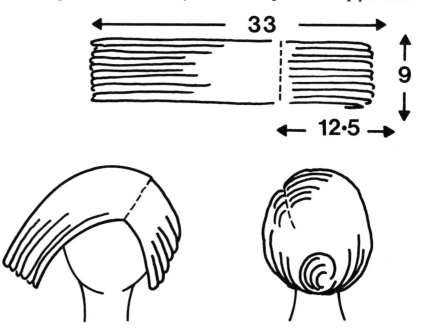

Fig 47 Annette, showing construction of hair. All measurements given in centimetres. (9cm = 3½in, 12.5cm = 5in, 33cm = 13in)

first testing on a spare piece of stockinette. Finally blush the cheeks (see Fig 48).

The clothes   *Ballet dress:* This costume is made in two parts. The underpart is the panties and bodice combined while the second part is the tulle skirt. Cut the bodice and pants from pink taffeta. If you cut two and sew them together, it will save you from hemming all the curved edges and also make a neater finish. Place the two pieces right sides together and sew along the entire upper and lower edge. Turn right side out and press. Turn under seam allowance on both sides of the centre back and slip stitch the edges together.

Fig 48   Facial features for Annette

The bodice can now be folded to sew the various seams that need joining. Since you have already used the seam allowance to neaten the edges just oversew the neatened edges together with tiny stitches. Join shoulder seams, lower half of the centre back seam and the between-legs or crotch seam. Close undergarment with a hook and eye at the top of the centre back opening. Ease neck to fit, gathering up if necessary. Sew floral braid or guipure daisies around the neck edge.

Cut the tulle into three equal sized strips across the width of the fabric. Lay strips on top of each other and gather all three together along one edge to make the waist. Fit on to doll to determine size then fasten off by sewing a hook and eye on to waist end of skirt. Decorate waist gathers with floral braid. Make shoulder straps by cutting swansdown in half and sewing each strap on to skirt at both front and back making two armholes (see Fig 49). Dress skirt on doll and pull layers of tulle apart.

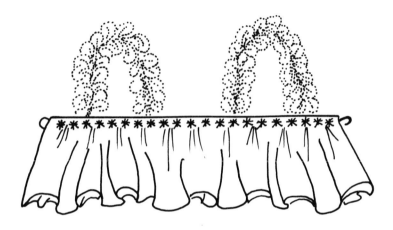

Fig 49   Annette, showing construction of the ballet skirt

Ballet shoes: Sew back heel edges of shoe together. Hem top edge. Cut card soles to the size of the pattern and taffeta soles slightly larger. Make soles as you did for the feet and fit to the shoes, easing in any fullness at the toes. Put shoes on doll and hold in place by sewing on pink ribbon straps, winding them around the ankle to hide the join to the leg.

Some more ideas for pivot-jointed dolls

1.   The wire and metal discs used to joint the limbs of Norman can be replaced by strong thread and buttons.
2.   The clothes for Mandy will fit Norman so make a pair of dolls and dress them as Jack and Jill.
3.   Enlarge the pattern for Gerry and make up using disc joints on the limbs or strong thread and buttons.

10 Useful dolls

Fashion houses, fortune tellers and film companies have all exploited dolls in some manner. Indeed it would be virtually impossible to indicate the complete range of uses, but probably the hey day of inventiveness was reached during the Victorian era. Dressed as crinoline ladies they were used to cover teapots and telephones and became a necessary part of household décor. The Victorian mother also saw the educational value of dolls in developing social graces and skills.

The dolls in this chapter represent only a limited fraction of this range but they can be used by children of all ages to keep their night clothes and sewing aids tidy. Wendy will help small children develop the physical skills needed to cope with the fastenings on their clothes.

Sleepy Sue

Height: 70cm (28in)
Plate 6: pattern graph 17

During the last hundred years nightdress cases in the form of soft toy animals and dolls have become increasingly popular. Although they are much loved by children as cuddly toys, adults use them largely as a decorative feature on their beds.

Sleepy Sue is made to either lie on the bed or hang from a knob. Her dress is the bag for holding the nightclothes.

Materials for doll 50cm (18in) calico; 226g (8oz) stuffing; 28g (1oz) double knitting wool for hair; small pieces of blue and white felt for face; pink and blue embroidery thread.

Materials for clothes 1m (39in) printed cotton; 23cm (9in) square felt for slippers; 20cm (8in) zip; 2.5m (8ft) lace; 14cm (5½in) by 32cm (12½in) strong card.

The doll *Head:* The head for Sleepy Sue is the same pattern as used for Arabella (see page 63) except that the neck edge is extended. Make up in exactly the same way as for Arabella. Finish off by folding in opposite sides of the neck and stitching the flaps down rather than by gathering.
Facial features: Sew blue felt circles on for eyes. Use a lighter blue embroidery thread to work double crosses across the eye. The cheeks are white felt circles held down with pink double crosses. Using the

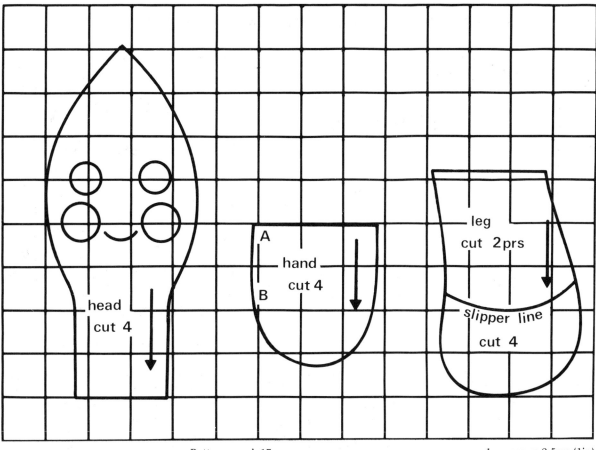

Pattern graph 17   1 square = 2.5cm (1in)

same pink thread, work two straight stitches for the nostrils and a stem stitch mouth.

Hair: Cut wool into 60cm (23in) lengths. Sew a central parting that is 12cm (5in) wide. Attach wool to head by back stitching through the parting. Pull hair down to frame the face on either side and stitch in place on a line level with the base of the cheeks.

Legs and slippers: Cut four felt slippers from the leg pattern then baste one to each leg. Sew legs together in pairs and turn right side out leaving top straight edge open. Stuff each leg nearly to the top and baste the open edges together. Put legs aside for the moment.

Arms: These are made with the sleeves.

The clothes   *Nightdress:*   Cut the nightdress by following the measurements given in Figure 50. Bring the two selvedge edges together and sew, inserting the zip in the middle of the seam. This seam becomes the centre back of the nightdress. Insert legs into bottom opening of nightdress on either side of the back seam and sew right across the bottom edge (see Fig 51). Open out the bottom edge by pulling front and back apart on either side at the points marked by an X on Figure 51. Sew across each corner making a 12cm (5in) wide seam. Fold points in towards feet and catch them down on the seam (see Fig 51).

Shape the card base by rounding off the corners. Cut a piece of calico slightly larger than the card. Gather up the edge of the calico enclosing the card. Place covered card base in nightdress and catch down at the sides and on to the centre back seam. Sew a layer of lace along the bottom edge of the nightdress. Turn under the top edge of the nightdress and make a 2.5cm (1in) deep hem. Gather up neck

97

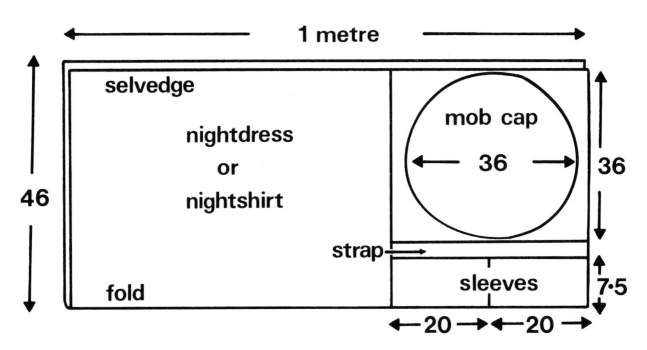

Fig 50 Pattern layout for Sleepy
Sue. Cut nightdress (or nightshirt)
and sleeves on the fold, hat and
strap from double fabric and
discard one strap. Measurements
given in centimetres. (7.5cm = 3in,
20cm = 8in, 36cm = 14in,
46cm = 18in)

edge at base of the neck hem and sew very securely to the neck
stump of the head.

Arms and sleeves: Sew two hand pieces together from A to B then
open out and sew wrist edge to base of a sleeve. Fold arm in half
lengthways and sew from B around curved edge of hand and up long
edge of sleeve. Leave top edge open. Turn arm right side out and
stuff. Close top opening by turning in raw edges. Position arm on
side of nightdress and hem in place. Make second arm in same way.
Sew lace around wrists.

Mob cap: Sew the two circles of fabric together around the edge
leaving a small opening. Turn right side out and close opening. Hem
lace around edge. Gather up cap along a line 4cm (1½in) in from the
edge. Fit cap on head and back stitch to head along the gathering
line. Fold the strap in half and sew the long edges together. Turn
right side out and press. Fold strap in half to make a loop and sew
securely to the top of the mob cap.

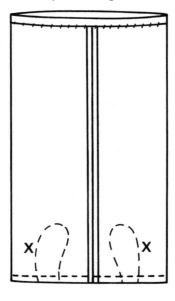

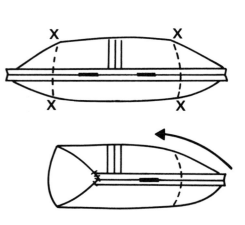

Figure 51 Sleepy Sue showing
construction of nightdress case

98

Wee Willie Winkie

Height: 80cm (31½in)
Plate 6; pattern graph 17

Wee Willie Winkie is a pyjama case for little boys. He is made in exactly the same way as Sleepy Sue, page 96, using the same pattern pieces, but wears a nightcap instead of the mob cap. Choose a striped cotton to make his nightshirt and cap.

The doll Make as for Sleepy Sue but use half the amount of wool to make shorter hair. Make a fringe as in Figure 52 and stitch this around the head from side to side. Trim to shape after the cap has been sewn on. Embroider light-brown french knots over his face for freckles and omit the white felt cheeks.

The clothes *Nightshirt:* Make as for Sleepy Sue but leave out the card base and do not use any lace for decoration. Cut a calico bib and top stitch this to the front of the shirt. Sew on three fancy buttons.
Nightcap: Cut the nightcap from the area of fabric set aside for the mob cap. Figure 53 shows the measurements and the finished cap. Stitch both sides together and hem the straight edge. Sew loop on to top of cap by catching in a small fold and sewing on the wrong side. Make a wool tassel and attach to point of cap. Back stitch cap on to head through the hem line.

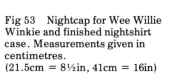

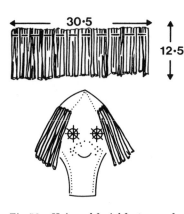

Fig 52   Hair and facial features of Wee Willie Winkie. Measurements given in centimetres.
(12.5cm = 5in, 30.5cm = 12in)

Fig 53   Nightcap for Wee Willie Winkie and finished nightshirt case. Measurements given in centimetres.
(21.5cm = 8½in, 41cm = 16in)

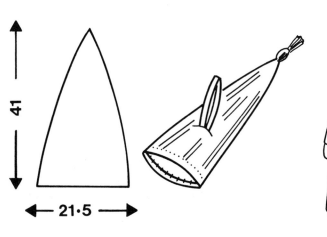

Wendy

Height: 60cm (24in)
Plates 1 and 6; pattern graphs 8 and 18

Wendy is a double-hinged doll, the body being made from the same pattern as Arabella (see page 63). On this occasion she is wearing a set of clothes that incorporate a variety of fastenings such as buttons, zip, buckle, laces and bows. Dressing Wendy will quickly teach a little girl how to cope with the fastenings on her own clothes.

Materials for doll

Calico as for Arabella to make the body, legs and feet; 84g (3oz) double knitting wool for hair; embroidery threads for face; colouring for cheeks.

Materials for clothes

61cm (24in) small-print cotton; 61cm (24in) plain colour cotton; 30.5cm (12in) square black felt; 2m (2yd) russia braid; 107cm (42in) narrow elastic; 107cm (42in) Broderie Anglaise; 10cm (4in) zip; 2.5cm (1in) belt buckle; 3 beads for purse; 3 buttons for blouse; 1 snap fastener; 10 eyelets; hair ribbons; one pair of knee-length baby socks.

The doll

Body: Follow the pattern and instructions for making Arabella remembering to make legs and feet from calico.
Facial features: Outline the eyes and work eyelashes with a dark brown or tan colour stem stitch. The eyes are worked in light-blue stem stitch while the pupils are navy blue stem stitch. Work mouth in stem stitch and then blush the cheeks with colouring. Finally, work a few white stitches in the pupils as highlights (see Fig 54).
Hair: Cut all the wool into lengths of 1m (39in). Spread them out and sew a central parting 18cm (7in) wide. Back stitch hair on to head through the parting. Glue wool to head and catch down at sides and nape of neck. Divide wool into two equal-sized bundles and plait each bundle in turn. Tie a ribbon on the end of each plait and trim odd lengths of wool.

Fig 54   Facial features for Wendy

The clothes

Pants: Make these in printed cotton, decorating the leg edges with Broderie Anglaise. You will find the pattern on the pattern graph for Arabella, page 63, it is for a shorter pair of pants that only reach the knees. Follow the instructions given for Arabella to make the pants.
Blouse: Make the blouse in the printed cotton. Sew fronts to back on the shoulder seams. Hem the wrist edge of each sleeve and decorate with Broderie Anglaise. Work a row of gathering or zigzag on the elastic guide-line. Gather the head of the sleeve to ease up the fullness then insert in armhole opening and sew. Sew underarm and sides together in one continuous seam. Finish other sleeve in same way.

Hem waist edge of blouse. Turn under front edges and hem. Neaten neck with a bias strip of printed cotton. Close neck with a snap fastener and work three buttonholes down the front. Sew on three buttons to finish the blouse.
Pinafore: Make the pinafore in plain-coloured cotton and neaten the edges with bias strips of printed cotton. Start by sewing fronts to backs on the shoulders. Neaten armholes and neck edge after first ironing down the centre front seam allowance. Sew the centre front seam below the zip opening. Insert zip in top of centre front seam. Sew both side seams. Cut a frill for the bottom of the pinafore

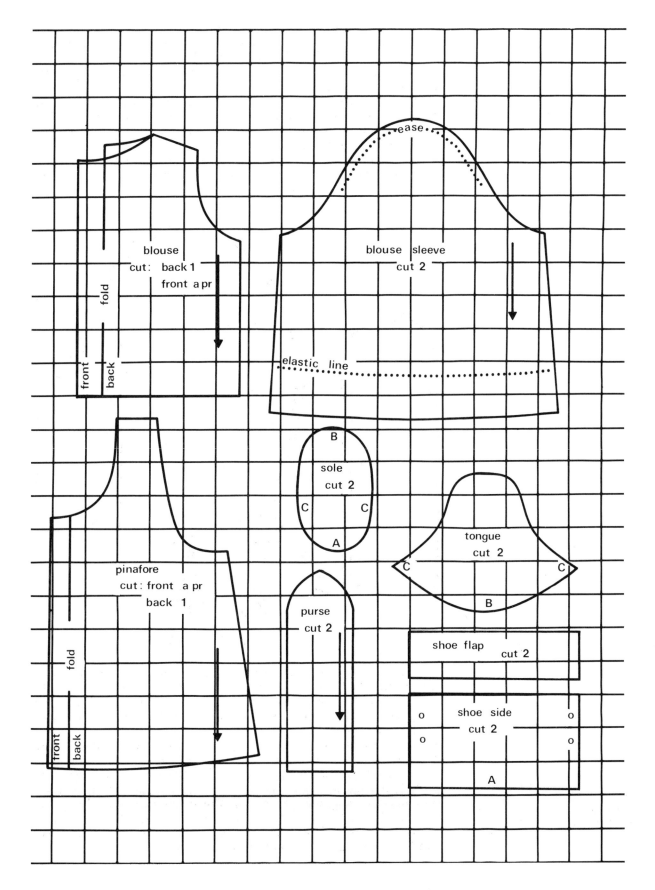

blouse
cut: back 1
front a pr

fold

front
back

blouse sleeve
cut 2

ease

elastic line

pinafore
cut: front a pr
back 1

fold

front
back

sole
cut 2

B

C   C

A

purse
cut 2

tongue
cut 2

C   C

B

shoe flap
cut 2

shoe side
cut 2

o   o

o   o

A

Pattern graph 18

1 square = 2.5cm (1in)

measuring 138cm (54in) by 11cm (4½in). Join strips to make the correct length. Hem bottom edge of frill then gather top edge to fit bottom of pinafore. Sew short ends of frill together and then sew frill to pinafore. A piping of printed cotton between the frill and pinafore makes an interesting feature.

Belt: Cut a strip of plain-coloured cotton 40cm (16in) by 5cm (2in). Fold in half widthways and sew the long edges together. Turn belt right side out and press. Attach one end to a buckle and neaten the free end into a point. Make two eyelets in the belt.

Purse: Place pieces of purse right sides together and sew round all edges leaving a small opening. Turn right side out, close opening and press. Fold purse as in Figure 55 and sew to shape the bottom.

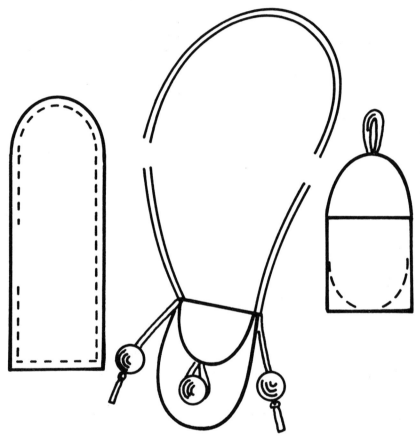

Fig 55   Purse for Wendy

Trim away excess fabric. Turn right side out. Make a loop from russia braid to fit the bead. Sew loop to closing flap and bead to centre front of purse. Make shoulder straps from same braid and leave the ends hanging on either side. Thread a bead on each end and knot to hold in place.

Shoes: Sew side to sole matching A to A. Now sew tongue to sole matching B to B and C to C on each side. The ends of the tongue piece, C, will overlap the ends of the side piece. Place the right side of the flap to the wrong side of the shoe side and sew a narrow seam. Now make eyelets on the shoe at the position marked O on the pattern. Turn shoe right side out and put on foot over the sock. Cut a length of russia braid and lace the shoe. Knot the ends of the braid and then tie a bow. Make second shoe in same way.

102

Fig 56   Plastic bottles suitable for making either Jane or Julia

Jane

Height: 30cm (12in)
Plate 6; pattern graph 19

Victorian mothers anxious to encourage their young daughters in fine sewing lost no opportunity in making use of china dolls as pin-cushions and Worktable Companions. These were sewing dolls that held pins, needles, thimble, scissors and as many other sewing aids as could possibly be incorporated into the clothing. The legs of the doll were often removed so that the skirt could be filled with sand and thus used as a pincushion.

Jane is constructed around an empty plastic bottle that has been made stable by the addition of sand or similar heavy substance. There are many different styles of plastic bottle suitable for making this doll. It is, therefore, impossible to give exact measurements for clothing and consequently emphasis is placed more on the way it is constructed.

Materials for doll A plastic shampoo bottle that has 'shoulders and waist', as in Figure 56; sand, sawdust or rice to weight the bottle; 2 pipe cleaners for arms; 56g (2oz) stuffing; nylon stocking; 2 small black beads for eyes; cheek colouring; a skein of embroidery thread for hair.

Materials for clothes Fabric with small floral print to make dress; felt, ribbon and lace for bonnet; cotton and lace for petticoat; white cotton, lace, snap fastener and flannelette for apron; basket, velvet, stuffing and hook and eye for pincushion basket.

The doll *Body:* Remove and discard lid of bottle. Half-fill bottle with sand and plug neck with stuffing. Cut a 15cm (6in) length of stocking leg and knot in the middle. Push a small handful of stuffing up one end of tube against the knot. Tie up tightly beneath stuffing so that you have a golf-ball-sized head. Twist both ends of stocking tube around neck of bottle and tie securely in place.
Facial features: Needle-model the face to form a nose, mouth and eye sockets. Outline the eyes and eyebrows with small, dark-coloured running stitches and sew beads in sockets as eyeballs. Very carefully colour the cheeks and mouth with moistened pencil.
Hair: Remove labels from embroidery skein and sew a central parting to hold skein in place. Lay hair on head and glue in position, pulling down on each side to frame the face. Fasten ends down behind head.

The clothes *Petticoat:* Place bottle centrally on circle of petticoat fabric. Gather up edge, pull up to waist of bottle and fasten off (see Fig 57). Decorate hem edge with lace.
Dress: Cut a tube to fit upper part of bottle as bodice. Turn under neck edge and gather on to bottle. Neaten neck with lace or collar. Cut a rectangle for the skirt, make a centre back seam, hem the edge then gather on to waist of bottle.
Arms and sleeves: Fold pipe cleaner to make lower arm and hand shape (see Fig 58). Pull a small piece of stocking tightly over hand and bind off at wrist. Hem sleeve edge and sew underarm seam. Turn sleeve right side out. Push arm and hand down sleeve to expose hand. Stuff upper arm loosely then sew top of sleeve neatly on to shoulder. Make second arm and sleeve in the same way.

Plate 8   NOVELTY DOLLS
Left to right Louisa, Caroline, Joe

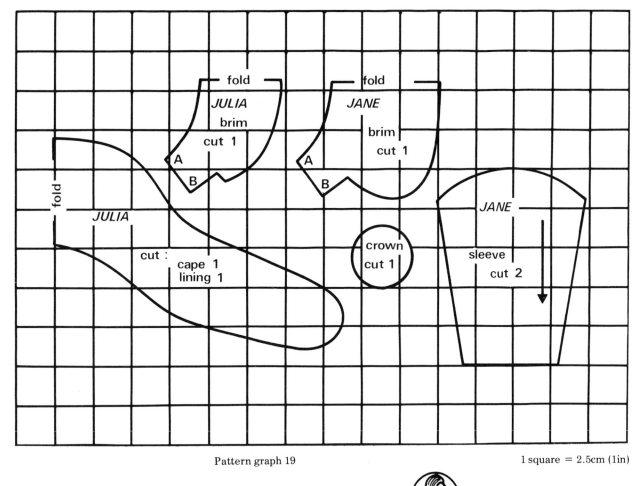

Pattern graph 19

1 square = 2.5cm (1in)

Fig 57   Method of forming Jane's petticoat around plastic bottle

Fig 58   Method of making hand and lower arm of Jane

Bonnet: Join centre back seam A to B by oversewing. Insert crown matching A to A and oversew. Turn bonnet right side out and put on head. Cut to fit, or stuff crown if necessary. Turn brim back, decorate with lace and ribbon. Make bow under chin.

Basket: Cut an oval of velvet. Run a gathering thread around the edge and pull up. Stuff firmly before closing off. Push velvet ball into basket and decorate with pins.

Apron: Cut apron approximately 12cm (5in) long by 10cm (4in) wide. Hem edges. Make a pocket large enough to hold a thimble. Put apron on to a waistband and fasten off at back with a snap fastener. Cut a piece of flannelette the same size as the apron and sew to the waistband under the apron. Put needles in the flannelette. Sew a hook on to the hand of the doll and an eye on to the waistband. Place basket on arm then fasten hand to waistband.

Julia

Height: 28cm (11in)
Plate 6; pattern graph 19

Julia is another sewing aid doll made basically like Jane but with a few significant differences. Her face is a stockinette mask while her arms are a continuous stuffed tube that extends from shoulder to shoulder. She wears a cape to carry needles on the underside of the flaps and a fur muff to hold pins.

Take a mask from a modern teenage fashion doll for quickness. Soak two pieces of stockinette in wallpaper paste then smooth each one in turn on to the face. As the mask is drying out, you will need to press around the eye sockets, nostrils and mouth with a toothpick. This will help to keep the features sharp. Make the head in the same way as for Jane and sew the dry mask on to the front. Use moistened coloured pencils to draw facial features.

Make a tube for the arms, insert two pipe cleaners and then stuff the tube loosely. Sew both ends on to respective shoulders and bend pipe cleaners to form elbows. Fold a piece of white fur around the centre of the tube to form a muff. Cut a cape from felt and a lining from flannelette. Sew them together. Drape the cape around shoulders, under the muff and arrange the flaps neatly in front. A small hanging bag could hold a thimble.

Some more ideas for useful dolls

1.   Doll shapes can be useful as playmats, sleeping bags and cushions.
2.   Design a cape and hood with toggle fastenings to dress Wendy as Little Red Riding Hood,
3.   Make a fun costume for Wendy that has numbers and letters of the alphabet appliquéd on to a long dress.
4.   Use the bottle doll construction to make a series of historical costumed dolls.
5.   Face masks set in the centre of felt flowers make useful needle-cases, see Figure 59.

6. Make a very large doll that can wear its owner's clothes.
7. Sew pockets on the skirt of Jane or Julia to hold additional items like tape measure and threads.

Fig 59   A felt needlecase in the form of a flower doll

11 Rainy day dolls

Many countries have simple traditional dolls that are made from materials which are readily available. Thus wood and leaves are frequently used, as are clay and soft rocks which can easily be moulded and carved. Until quite recently the use of cloth was more restricted as it was both scarce and costly and therefore rather precious.

In contrast cloth is now readily available and it is possible to develop and even reinterpret many of these traditional forms using fabric. Such an exercise should be a test for your ingenuity providing an opportunity to develop simple patterns and methods of construction.

Collected together in this chapter are a group of dolls that require very little in the way of pattern pieces or even knowledge of traditional doll-making. Nor do they need any special fabrics, as they are made from remnants, odd socks and even old, but clean, tights. They are simple dolls, quick to start and are therefore ideal for introducing young children to doll-making on a rainy day.

Lucy

Height: 20cm (8in)
Plate 7

An odd sock, no matter what the size, can soon be made into a delightful baby doll dressed in a snow-suit. The addition of a piece of stockinette for the head or a face mask is often all that is needed apart from scraps of wool, ribbon or braid. The three sock-doll examples that follow are all dressed as winter babies in snow-suits. Lucy and the Twins are soft, cuddly sitting babies while Tony is filled with rice and consequently is poseable.

Materials for doll One brightly coloured adult's ankle length sock; either make or purchase a face mask approximately 9cm (3½in) long; 56g (2oz) stuffing; white fur and white pompoms to finish snow-suit.

The doll Cut the toe off the sock to make the arms. Press foot of sock flat and slit to form the legs (see Fig 60). Sew legs on wrong side, turn sock right side out and stuff up to the ankle edge. Gather up and fasten off. Cut toe vertically to make two arms and then sew these on to the sides of the body. The heel of the sock becomes the bottom of the sitting baby. Sew face mask in place then cover edges by framing with a strip of rolled fur. Make wool pompoms to tie around neck.

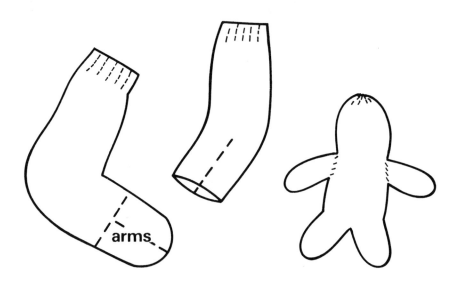

Fig 60   Pattern for making Lucy
from a sock

The wrists can be shaped by stitching a gathering thread around the arms and pulling up.

The Twins

Height: 14cm (5½in)
Plate 7

Choose a pair of child's white lacy socks, size 3 to 5. Cut the toe off to make arms and the ribbing to make a snow hat (see Fig 61). Cut a strip of stockinette, seam into a tube and sew on to neck end of sock. Slit body to form legs. Sew legs, stuff body and close head by gathering up the stockinette. Also gather neck to give more shaping. Cut toe vertically to make two arms, sew, stuff and stitch on to body. Make hat by gathering up tightly, the cut end. Embroider blue

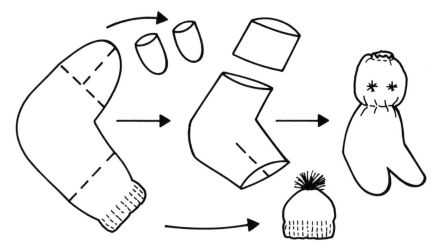

Fig 61   Pattern for making a twin
from a sock

double cross stitches for eyes. Finish girl twin with pink ribbon and pompom and boy twin with blue ribbon and pompom.

Tony

Height: 24cm (9½in)
Plate 7

This little sock baby is constructed so that he can stretch out full length. In addition he is filled with rice, which makes his body completely poseable. Tony has a purchased face mask 6cm (2½in) long and braid to decorate his snow-suit.

Choose an adult's brightly coloured ankle-length sock. Cut the foot off just behind the heel (see Fig 62). Slit the ankle edge to form legs, sew, turn right side out and stuff legs and body with rice. Use soft stuffing for the head. Gather up heel edge which now becomes the back of the head. Sew on face mask. Cut toe of sock in half vertically to make arms, sew, fill with rice and attach to body. Make a pixie hood from the remaining portion of sock. Place hood on head to frame face and hide edge of mask, stitch to neck. Cover neck join with braid and continue braid down front of snow-suit.

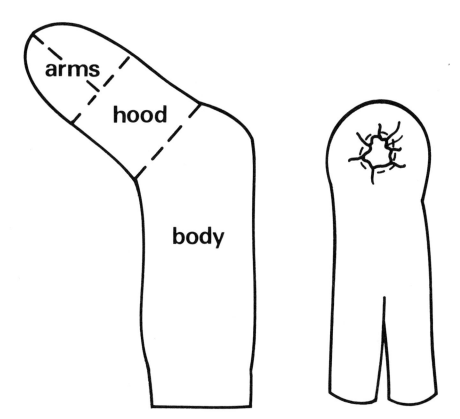

Fig 62   Pattern for making Tony from a sock

Suffolk Maid

Height: 15cm (6in)
Plate 7

Here is an opportunity to use up small remnants of cotton fabric and make an unusual stretchy doll. The dress is made from circles of fabric which are first gathered around the edge then pressed flat. It is a patchwork technique used for making Suffolk puffs but whereas in patchwork they are used flat, toy-makers thread them on elastic, building the puffs up one upon another to make bodies and limbs.

Materials for doll 15cm (6in) square flesh-coloured felt; 28g (1oz) stuffing; two pipe cleaners; a skein of doll's mohair for wig; black fibre-tip pen; white and red Sylko.

Materials for clothes Remnants of cotton totalling 80cm (31in); 23cm (9in) millinery elastic; 2 large flat buttons; lace trimming; ribbon for hair; strong card.

The doll *Head:* Cut a circle of flesh-coloured felt 10cm (4in) in diameter and shape into a ball by gathering the edge and enclosing stuffing in the centre before pulling up and fastening off. Place the gathers at the back of the head where the wig will cover them.
Facial features: Use black pen and draw eyes and dots for the nostrils. The mouth consists of three tiny, red straight stitches while the highlights of the eyes are two small, white straight stitches.
Hair: Spread a layer of glue over the head and press mohair wig on, framing the face. Collect into a ponytail with a ribbon after the Maid has been assembled.
Arms and hands: Cut 4 small mitten-shaped pieces of felt and stitch together in pairs. Turn right side out and cover both ends of

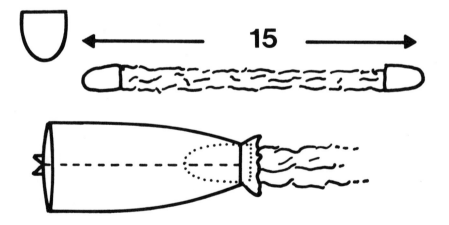

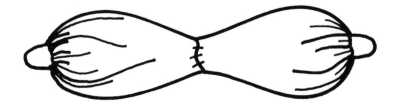

Fig 63 Method of making arm and sleeve for Suffolk Maid. Measurements given in centimetres. (15cm = 6in)

112

pipe cleaners with a mitten (see Fig 63). Cut sleeves measuring 10cm (4in) by 6cm (2½in), seam long edges together and while still inside out, push each sleeve over a hand and bind on to the wrists (see Fig 63). Pull sleeves back towards shoulders and stitch together in the centre. Put aside while you make the dress puffs.

The clothes

Dress: Circles of fabric the following sizes are needed to make the dress:

> four at 19cm (7½in) in diameter
> five at 16.5 cm (6½in) in diameter
> five at 14cm (5½in) in diameter
> one at 11.5 cm (4½in) in diameter

In addition you will need two circles of card each measuring 9cm (3½in) in diameter.

Turn under the raw edge of a large fabric circle and run a gathering thread around the edge (see Fig 64). Before pulling up, place both pieces of card centrally on the wrong side of the fabric then tie a button in the middle of the elastic and place button centrally on the card. Pull up gathering thread so that the fabric circle closes around the card and button (see Fig 64). This foundation puff makes a flat base for the doll to stand on.

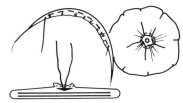

Fig 64 Preparation of puffs for the Suffolk Maid. The foundation puff is shown with card and button enclosed in the puff

Fig 65 Suffolk Maid showing the arrangement of puffs. Measurements given in centimetres. (11.5cm = 4½in, 14cm = 5½in, 16.5cm = 6½in, 19cm = 7½in)

1x11·5

5x14

5x16·5

4x19

Prepare all the Suffolk puffs, except the smallest one, by gathering the edge, drawing up tightly and fastening off. Flatten the puffs between your fingers to make discs then pierce the centre of each one by pushing a steel knitting needle between the gathers and out through the smooth side (see Fig 64).

The puffs are now ready to be assembled on the elastic threads which are anchored in the foundation puff. Push the two free ends of elastic through the central hole of each puff from the gathered side. Figure 65 shows the arrangement of the puffs. Tie the ends of elastic together through the second button and then gather up the smallest circle, enclosing the button, and fasten off.

Pass the arms between the two elastic strands beneath the second puff. Slip stitch the second and third puffs together at front and back and over the sleeves to hold the arms in place. Hide stitches with a row of lace and sew a second row of lace around the hem line. Ladder stitch head to the top puff and bend arms into a pleasing position.

Hat: Cut two fabric circles 11.5cm (4½in) in diameter. Sew them right sides together around the edge leaving a small opening. Turn right side out, close opening and press. Gather up 12mm (½in) from the edge to make a mob cap. Fit on head and sew in place.

Humpty Dumpty

Height: 25cm (10in)
Plate 7; pattern graph 20

Mascots are a well established part of the soft toy or doll industry with fiction, films and television all playing a part in popularizing the characters. Teddy bears, Walt Disney heroes and heroines, Noddy, Little Women, Alice in Wonderland and Florence are all examples, as are the characters that dangle from the back of car windows.

Humpty Dumpty is perhaps one of the most successful mascot dolls, having remained popular for a long time. With his longer-than-usual legs and extra bushy hair he is reminiscent of the Gonks that were fashionable as mascots during the 1960s.

Materials for doll

15cm (6in) gingham; 23cm (9in) velvet; 112g (4oz) stuffing; small pieces of felt for eyes, nose and shoes; 14g (½oz) double knitting wool for hair.

The doll

Head: Sew two gingham head pieces together along one curved edge then sew the other two together in the same way. Place both sets of head pieces together and sew both curved edges.
Body: Make the body in the same way as the head.
Arms: Sew a gingham hand to the bottom of each arm. Sew arms and hands together in pairs, turn right side out and stuff to within 2.5cm (1in) of the top. Baste arms centrally to straight edges of body sides. Place right sides of head and body together with all seams matching. Sew around the middle from side to side, leaving an opening between the two back segments. Turn Humpty Dumpty right side out and check that arms are secure. Stuff body firmly and close opening.

114

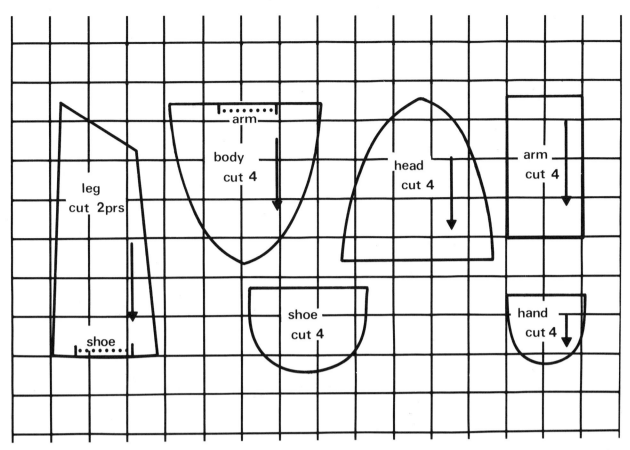

Pattern graph 20   1 square = 2.5cm (1in)

Legs: These are made in the same way as those for Rodriguez except that the trouser leg has a seam on each side. Stuff legs up to 2.5cm (1in) from the top, turn in the seam allowance then ladder stitch legs to body on either side.

Face: Cut felt shapes for eyes, stab stitch them together then hem to face. Gather up circle, 5cm (2in) in diameter, for nose, enclose stuffing before closing then ladder stitch to face.

Hair: Cut approximately 60 strands of wool each 15cm (6in) long. Tie the strands together in three separate bundles then stitch each bundle to the head. Glue in place and when dry, trim.

Rebecca

Height: 46cm (18in)
Plates 1 and 7

Dressed in all her finery, this young North African lady belies the simplicity of her construction. Her body consists of no more than two very quickly made plaits and a ball of stuffing for the head. Indeed, the clothes and jewellery will take longer to make than the body.

Materials for doll   3 pairs of tights; 170g (6oz) stuffing; 2 black buttons for eyes; 28g

115

(1oz) black poodle wool; a packet of macramé beads for hair; 30.5cm (12in) square of stockinette.

Materials for clothes   61cm (24in) black taffeta; 61cm (24in) narrow elastic; 1m (1yd) gaily printed cotton for caftan; 3m (3yd) russia braid for girdle; beads for necklace; curtain rings for bracelets and ear-rings.

The doll   *Arms and legs:*   Cut the legs off each pair of tights and knot three of the legs together at the toe end. This will become the hand of the doll. Plait the three legs together, tightly and evenly, taking care not to twist the plait. Tie a thread around the stockings where the plait ends, leaving about 5cm (2in) of the stocking legs unplaited to form a foot. Make another arm and leg plait from the remaining three legs, taking care to ensure that the two plaits are the same length. The hands are finished by folding the sides of the toes inwards and slip stitching the edges together. Shape the feet in the same way, folding in the sides and end of stockings until you have the right size and shape for a foot. Indicate toes by taking long, straight stitches over the edge and pulling up slightly to make each toe more prominent.

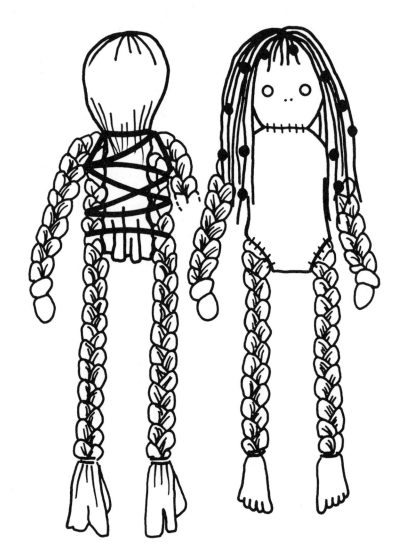

Fig 66   Rebecca showing construction of the body

Head: Place a large handful of stuffing in the centre of the stockinette and bind up tightly to form a ball about the size of an orange. The corners of stockinette hanging down from the ball form the neck and body stump. Cover the head with one or even two layers of tight fabric to get the correct colour 'skin' for the face.

Body: Place an arm and leg plait on either side of the body stump with correct proportions for length of each limb. Bind middle section of plaits to the body stump with wool. Take each remaining seat of tights and fold the long sides into the centre so that you have a band approximately 30.5cm (12in) long by 10cm (4in) wide. Stitch one short end of band to front neck edge, close up under the head. Pass the other end of the band between the legs and pull it up to the back neck edge and again stitch down. Catch the band on either side of the arms and then sew side seams together. Tuck in band to come diagonally across legs to crotch (see Fig 66).

Hair: Cut wool into 40cm (16in) lengths and tie together in several bundles rather than have a conspicuous parting. Sew bundles on to top of head. Cut fringe lengths for the front. Thread macramé beads on to wool strands and hold in place by knotting the wool. Glue hair down to head after making the face. Leave hair at random lengths to achieve the best effect.

Face: Sew on two black shiny buttons for eyes and work a small straight stitch or two for the nostrils.

The clothes

Pants: Cut two pieces of black taffeta each measuring 20cm (8in) by 23cm (9in). Assemble pants by following directions for the Box method (see p 30) making a 10cm (4in) centre front seam.

Petticoat: Cut a strip of black taffeta 91cm (36in) wide by 33cm (13in) long. Seam short ends together, hem bottom edge and make a casing for elastic on the waist edge. Fit pants and petticoat on to Rebecca.

Caftan: Make a pattern for the caftan by following the measurements in Figure 67. Cut the caftan with the upper arms and shoulders on a fold. Make neck opening by cutting a T. Hem the neck opening and wrist edges of sleeves then sew underarms and sides together, of each side, in one continuous seam. Hem lower edge and fit caftan on doll. Cut braid into three equal lengths and plait a girdle to fit around the waist. Leave the hanging ends unplaited. Tie girdle

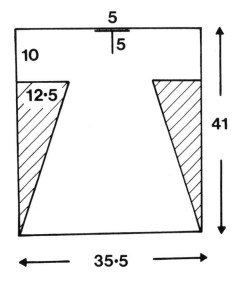

Fig 67   Pattern of caftan for Rebecca. Measurements given in centimetres.
(5cm = 2in, 10cm = 4in, 12.5cm = 5in, 35.5cm = 14in, 41cm = 16in)

around caftan. Finish Rebecca by sewing on bracelets and ear-rings, and make her a chunky necklace.

Ruth

Height: 23cm (9in)
Plate 7

Ruth is a smaller version of Rebecca, being made from one pair of tights. Cut one of the legs into three long strips, knot them together at one end and plait the entire length finishing with another knot. Neaten each end beyond the knots by folding in the strips, forming feet and stitching toes. Bend the plait to find halfway, then bind two wrists, each 2.5cm (1in) behind the bend. Cut the plait in the centre and turn in the cut ends to form hands with stitched fingers.

Using the second leg of the tights, cut a piece to tie around a ball of stuffing for the head. Use the remainder of the tights to fashion a body, binding in the neck stump from the head and the plaits between the legs and arms as directed for Rebecca (see Fig 66).

The hair is 50 strands of wool, each 17.5cm (7in) long. The bundle is tied in the middle and then stitched to the top of the head and stitched again around the nape of the neck to hold it in place. Sew two dark beads on the face as eyes.

The dress and pants are stitched permanently on to the body. The pants are a strip measuring 12.5cm (5in) by 5cm (2in) hemmed at top and bottom edges, seamed into a tube and then gathered on to the waist. The legs are separated by top stitching. Figure 68 shows the measurements of the dress and sleeves. Fold the sleeves widthways to save hemming them. Make a short shoulder seam on each side then sew sleeves on to sides. Sew underarm and side seams as one continuous seam on each side. Hem dress and fit on doll. Turn under neck edge and gather on to body. Ruth has her hands stitched together so that she can carry a small purchased basket.

Fig 68 Pattern of dress for Ruth and method of inserting sleeves. Measurements given in centimetres.
(5.5cm = 2¼in, 7.5cm = 3in, 8cm = 3¼in, 12.5cm = 5in)

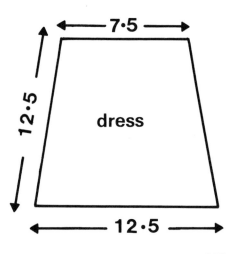

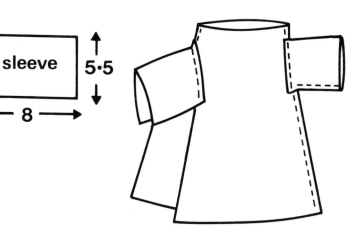

118

Some more ideas for rainy day dolls

1. Use a flesh-coloured knee-length sock to make a doll for dressing. White socks left overnight in a weak tea solution emerge with a light tan colour. Follow the instructions for Tony, making longer legs, embroidering a face and covering the gathers on the back of the head with hair. Fill with soft stuffing rather than beans or rice.

2. The Suffolk Maid constructed from white tulle puffs with halo and wings would make an angel for the Christmas tree.

3. A different style of doll can be made by forming a cone of either buckram, Vilene, felt or even card and inserting the tip of the cone into a ball head. Pipe cleaners pushed through the cone make foundation arms.

4. Instead of using nylon tights to make plaits, try ribbons, french knitting, tubes of fabric and even strips of rag with raw edges turned inwards.

5. Figure 69 shows a selection of further ideas.

Fig 69 Some more ideas for simply made dolls.
Left to right a peasant couple made from fabric strips as tassel dolls; a cone and ball maiden; a clown with Suffolk puff limbs and a Burmese coil doll. The head of this doll is made by coiling ribbon while the limbs are lengths of ribbon with beads for hands and feet

12 Novelty dolls

Manufacturers are constantly on the look-out for different ways of presenting dolls. Features that were once new and quite novel are now commonplace. Indeed moving eyes have been in existence since the early seventeenth century while mechanisms for talking, crying, feeding, wetting nappies, walking and swimming have only been incorporated in commercial products during the last one hundred and fifty years.

All these mechanical innovations are characteristic of wood, china, bisque and plastic dolls; a different kind of approach is needed to make novelty, non-mechanical cloth dolls. Amongst the earliest examples were turnover or topsy turvy dolls that had long skirts hiding a second doll underneath and turnabout dolls with hats covering alternative heads. Nevertheless even these were adaptations from earlier bisque doll novelties.

The novelties provided by the dolls in this chapter are more concerned with their construction than with their activities, although slight variations of the tube doll principle can greatly extend its versatility as a play doll. Louisa is based on the boudoir dolls popular with adults as fashion items during the 1930s. Her dress is both made and decorated with patchwork. Whereas she can be considered delicate and beautiful, Joe is in direct contrast. His bruised, defeated look comes from a soft-sculptured and needle-modelled body, a technique which is both challenging and exciting because of the often unexpected results.

Caroline

Height: 69cm (27in)
Plate 8; pattern graph 21

Caroline is a doll without a conventional body. Her hands and feet are attached to either ends of two long continuous tubes which are then sewn together to make shoulders. The head is sewn on to the shoulders. The thickness and length of the tubes can be adapted to any size and still be used to construct this style of doll. Make the tubes from a stretch knitted fabric and you will be able to bend the limbs and even tie the legs in knots. Extremely long limbs filled with polystyrene granules will produce the same novel effect.

Materials for doll 15cm (6in) of 132cm (52in) wide furnishing-weight cotton for limbs; 23cm (9in) flesh-coloured fabric; 23cm (9in) by 46cm (18in) PVC for boots; 454g (1lb) stuffing; 56g (2oz) double knitting wool; embroidery threads for facial features; colouring for cheeks.

Materials for clothes 50cm (20in) wool tweed for costume; 2m (2¼yd) edging braid or

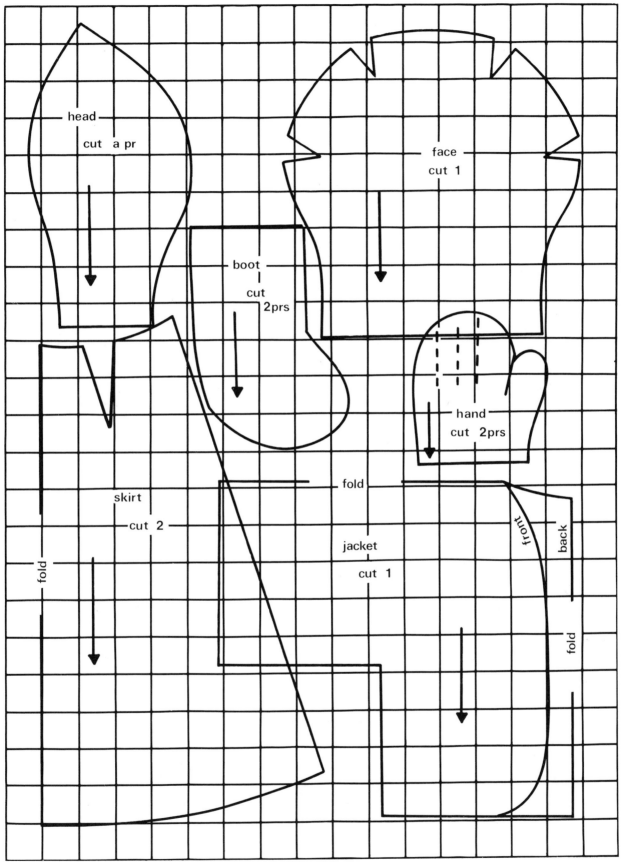

head
cut a pr

face
cut 1

boot
cut 2prs

hand
cut 2prs

skirt
cut 2

fold

fold

jacket
cut 1

front

back

fold

Pattern graph 21

1 square = 2.5cm (1in)

bias binding; two, 25cm (10in) squares of taffeta for combinations; 23cm (9in) narrow elastic; hooks and eyes; hair ribbons.

The doll

Head: With right sides facing, sew the centre back seam of the head. Make the four darts on the face and then sew head front and back together leaving the neck straight edge open. Turn head right side out, stuff firmly and close by gathering up the neck and fastening off.

Facial features: Embroider the outline of the eyes and the eyebrows with a brown-coloured chain stitch. Fill in the irises with Brussels' eyelet and work satin-stitch pupils. A few white stitches will make highlights on the pupils. Embroider the mouth with satin stitch and use colouring to blush the cheeks. Put the head aside for the moment while you make the body.

Body and limbs: The body is composed of two tubes that extend into arms and legs. Cut four strips from the furnishing cotton each measuring 7.5cm (3in) by 66cm (26in). Stitch the thumbs before you slash between them and the fingers. Cut hands from flesh-coloured fabric and boots from PVC. Position a boot at one end of a body strip and a hand at the other end. Make sure that the thumb and toe both point in the same direction. Sew each in place.

Make another unit in the same way using a reversed hand and boot. Place both strips together and sew all around the edge leaving a 5cm (2½in) opening on the back edge, level with the shoulders (see Fig 70). The shoulder position is found by folding the tube so that one-third forms the arm and the remaining two-thirds make the body and leg. Slash the thumb from the fingers at this stage. Turn completed tube right side out and top stitch the finger divisions.

Fig 70   Caroline, showing tubes folded to form limbs and body

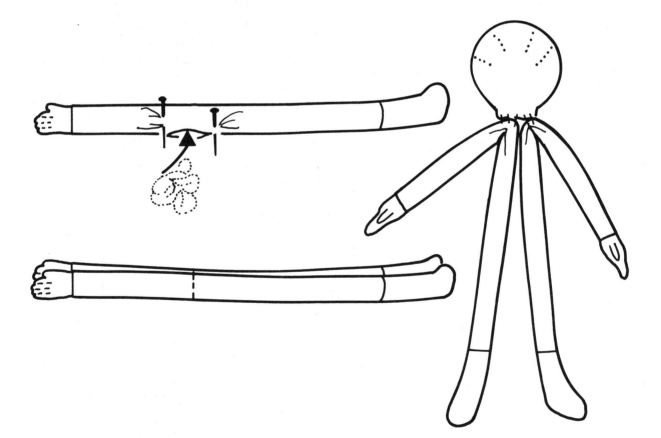

Stuff arm and leg carefully, avoiding any unsightly bumps. Hold stuffing away from both sides of the opening with pins. Make the second arm and leg tube in the same way. Close both openings with ladder stitch and then sew tubes together across the shoulder (see Fig 70). Ladder stitch the head to the completed body tubes. Work several rows of ladder stitch to ensure that they are joined securely.

Hair: Cut the wool into lengths of 82cm (32in). Reserve some strands for stitching the hair to the head and tying the ringlets. Spread the wool out and sew a central parting 18cm (7in) wide. Lay wool on head and back stitch to head through the central parting. Pull the hair down on either side of the face and stitch securely just above the neck. Divide the ends on each side into three equal bunches and twist into ringlets. Secure the ringlets, trimming the ends neatly and cover with a fancy bow on each side.

The clothes

Fig 71   Caroline, wearing combinations and showing method of construction. Measurements given in centimetres. (8cm = 3¼in)

Combinations: These are in effect a pair of pants with the upper part functioning as a sleeveless blouse. One square makes the front while the other becomes the back. Make a narrow hem along the bottom edge of both squares then fold over the top edge to make a 4cm (1½in) deep hem. Make another line of stitching 6mm (¼in) above the hemline thus forming a channel for the elastic (see Fig 71).

Place both squares right side together and sew 8cm (3in) side seams up from the lower edge on each side. Neaten the upper edges of each side, which now form the armholes. Thread elastic through the channel on the front, across the arm opening and through the back of the combinations. Measure the neck of the doll then cut elastic to size. Fasten off both ends of elastic and sew a hook and eye to either side of the open armhole on the shoulder. The legs of the pants are formed by top stitching a 5cm (2in) central division.

Jacket: Take particular care when preparing your pattern as the skirt and jacket overlap on the pattern graph. The pattern also allows for 12mm (½in) seams so that they can be neatened. Note the folds on the jacket which allow you to cut it out in one piece. Sew each underarm and side of jacket in one continuous seam. Clip the corner, hem sleeves then press. Finish jacket by sewing bias strip round the neck, front and lower edge.

Skirt: Make the darts on both front and back skirt pieces with narrow seams then sew the centre front and centre back seams, leaving a small waist opening at the back. Press seams open. Cut a waistband 30cm (12in) by 8cm (3in). Check skirt on doll for size before sewing to waistband. Neaten lower edge of skirt by covering with a wide bias strip. Finish skirt with hook and eye at back waist opening.

Louisa

Height: 54cm (21in)
Plate 8; pattern graph 22

This doll presents an opportunity to use several different types of patchwork. Her arms are in effect sleeves made from Suffolk puffs which are stitched directly on to the body through the bodice and for this reason Louisa cannot be dressed or undressed. Her body is similar in construction to the boudoir fashion dolls which women were encouraged to dress by the French couturier, Paul Poiret. These usually had face masks and were clothed in crêpes, silk or velvet. In the United States they were known as Vamps and Flappers while the English versions produced by Deans were the Smart Set and those produced by Chad Valley were known as Carnival Dolls or Sofa Dolls.

Materials for doll 50cm (18in) calico; 227g (8oz) stuffing; 56g (2oz) double knitting wool for hair; embroidery threads for face; coloured pencils for face; 13cm (5in) dowel rod, 12mm (½in) diameter for neck.

Materials for clothes 50cm (20in) cotton for skirt and bodice; 1.5m (1⅔yd) mixed cottons for patchwork; 61cm (24in) fabric for underwear; small piece of satin for slippers; satin ribbon and two pearl beads for rosettes; 4 flat buttons; 1m (1yd) millinery elastic; lace to trim clothes.

The doll *Body:* Seam front and back body together around all sides except lower edge. Cut top of neck off across line marked on pattern. Turn body right side out and stuff the shoulder and waist regions from the bottom opening. Put aside for the moment and make the legs.

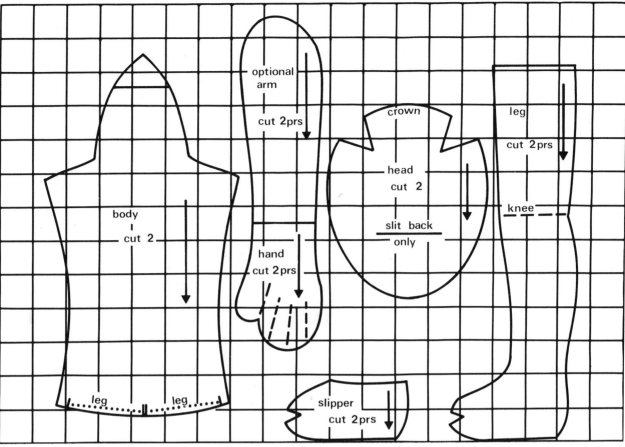

Pattern graph 22

1 square = 2.5cm (1in)

Legs: Sew small toe dart on each leg side then place legs together in pairs and sew leaving top, straight edge open. Turn leg right side out and stuff up to knee-hinge line. Press leg flat to bring front and back seams together in centre then top stitch across from side to side making the knee hinge. Finish stuffing leg, leaving top 2.5cm (1in) empty. Complete second leg in same way.

Turn under seam allowance on body, insert tops of legs, baste legs and body together then top stitch across from side to side catching legs securely in place.

Head: Make the two darts on either side of the crown for both front and back head pieces then sew head together leaving the crown open. Turn right side out and stuff firmly, being careful not to get too many crinkles in the chin. Select the best looking side for making the face and slit the back of the head as indicated on the pattern. The head is now ready to be joined to the body. Finish the body by pushing the stuffing well down and filling out the shoulders.

Insert the dowel rod through the neck and work it down into the stuffing until only 12mm (½in) projects from the neck. Finish stuffing the neck and close off by winding strong thread around cloth and dowel rod to fasten them securely together. Push your index finger through the slit on the back of the head and work a channel upwards to fit the neck — you may have to remove some stuffing from the head. Feed neck into head then ladder stitch together, using a long needle to sew under the chin from side to side.

Face: All the features are embroidered with stem stitch except the eyelashes which are straight stitches. The shading of the upper

125

Fig 72   Facial features for Louisa

eyelids, cheeks and mouth is done by using dry pencils. This keeps the colouring very soft and therefore only noticeable when you are next to Louisa. Figure 72 shows the outline of features.

Arm: An optional arm pattern complete with hand is given on the pattern graph. For Louisa you need only cut two pairs of hands as each arm is composed of 21 Suffolk puffs threaded on to millinery elastic.

To make the puffs, prepare a 15cm (6in) diameter card template and use this as your pattern to cut the 42 Suffolk puffs. Turn the outer edge of each puff under by 3mm (1/8in) and stitch a running thread around the edge. Pull up on thread, gather puff tightly and fasten off. Press flat between your fingers with gathered edge lying centrally. Pierce the centre, between the gathers, with a steel knitting needle. Lay puffs out in two similar piles and make the hands. Sew hands together in pairs, turn right side out and stuff. Stitch the finger divisions with stab stitch. Cut a 46cm (18in) length of millinery elastic and tie a button in the centre. Insert button into open end of hand and close hand around button to hold it in place leaving two ends of elastic hanging free. Thread 21 puffs on to elastic and then tie elastic off through a button. Make second arm in same way. Because the arms are sleeves as well they are stitched on to the bodice and not the body.

Hair: Wind wool into a 102cm (40in) skein and cut loops at one end only. Carefully lay wool across head so that 51cm (20in) falls on either side. Catch hair at centre front with self-coloured wool and take a few stitches across to the back. Back stitch hair down to nape of neck from side to side (see Fig 73).

Divide lengths of wool into ten equal bundles, five on each side of head. Working on one side at a time, and from the front, wind the first four bundles into four ringlets. You will find this easier to do if you clamp the doll between your knees. Straighten out the wool strands then twist evenly. (The method for forming ringlets is in the general instructions on hair-making, page 18.) Stitch the ends of each ringlet down to the head as near to the centre back as possible and on the underside out of sight. Curl the front ringlet into an 'ear-

Fig 73   Louisa, showing construction of ringlets and plaits

phone', this should help hide some of the ends. Stitch down. Pull the next ringlet forward over shoulder to hang down the front bodice. Make the four ringlets on the other side.

The remaining two bundles, one on either side of centre back, are each plaited. Use one plait to form the base of the coil and bring the second plait out through the centre to finish the top of the coil. Tuck ends of plaits inwards to centre. Figure 74 shows the finished hairstyle from the side.

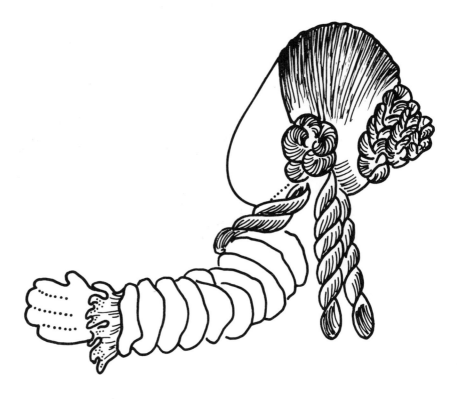

Fig 74   Louisa showing arm and finished hairstyle

The clothes

Pants: Cut two pieces measuring 18cm (7in) wide by 25cm (10in) long and make them up by following directions for the Box method, page 30, with a 13cm (5in) centre front and back seam. Decorate leg edges with lace and sew pants on to body without making an elasticated waistband.

Petticoat: Cut a strip for the petticoat measuring 33cm (13in) long by 91cm (36in) wide. Sew short sides together, hem lower edge and decorate with lace. Gather petticoat directly on to waist of doll and sew in place.

Dress: This consists of a skirt and bodice which are sewn on to the doll separately as well as the two sleeves with hands attached. Cut a skirt measuring 38cm (15in) long by 91cm (36in) wide. Sew short sides together and hem lower edge. Decorate border of skirt with some form of patchwork. Louisa's skirt has three rows of clamshell. The 'stems' are cut off the top row and the raw edges are covered by a band of double-sided Broderie Anglaise. Gather skirt on to waist of doll and stitch down securely. Cut a bodice measuring 13cm (5in) long by 30.5cm (12in) wide. Turn under top and bottom edges and wrap around chest of doll, turning in ends at back to make a centre back seam. Slip stitch edges together. Ladder stitch waist edge of bodice on to skirt, spreading any fullness evenly. Slip stitch front and back together on each shoulder for a short distance. Sew the uppermost Suffolk puff of an arm directly on to the bodice at the shoulder enclosing the button and ends of elastic. Sew other arm on in same way. Decorate wrist edges with gathered lace hanging down as a frill.

Slippers: Sew toe darts in each slipper piece then sew slippers together in pairs. Turn right side out and put on feet. Turn under top edges and slip stitch on to feet. Make each rosette by joining a satin ribbon into a tube then gathering up one edge and fastening off (see Fig 75). Sew pearl bead in centre and attach to front of slipper.

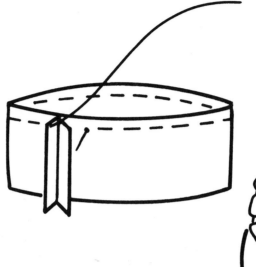

Fig 75   Preparation of rosette and slipper for Louisa

Joe

Height: 47cm (18½in)
Plate 8

Joe is surely the most unusual character in this chapter and indeed would not necessarily have universal appeal. His strong facial features and personality are formed by carefully stitching through a ball of stuffing covered with a layer of dishcloth cotton and nylon stocking. The face develops as you sew and place varying degrees of tension on each stitch. The features can then be further emphasized by embroidery, pencil or beads. This technique is referred to as soft sculpture with needle-modelling and the results depend entirely on one's personal creativity. Consequently no detailed patterns are given, only an outline of the methods employed.

Before you even start to make a soft-sculptured doll, try experimenting with stitches and tension on a ball of stuffing. You will be surprised at just how few stitches are needed. Use strong thread and work from side to side of nose or mouth, forming ridges, folds, sockets and dimples. Remember to look at the head from the side and the back, soft sculpture is a total effect, not just the face. Male characters will need ears. If you don't like the result, clip the thread, pull the stitches out and start again. Only practice will give you the confidence to make the face as you wish. Faces with strongly developed features make interesting and challenging subjects for this technique.

The rest of the body is made by wrapping stuffing around a wire framework and then covering the stuffing with a skin of nylon stocking. The arms for Joe have been made separately and then stitched in place on the shoulders. The hands have been needle-modelled to give definition to the fingers. The wire framework allows you to bend the limbs backwards and forwards to obtain the desired posture. You could also make a sitting model. The wire framework is shown in Figure 76. Remember to bind the cut ends with surgical or electrical adhesive tape. Dressmaker's weights or pieces of lead placed on the feet will provide a weighted base and increase stability.

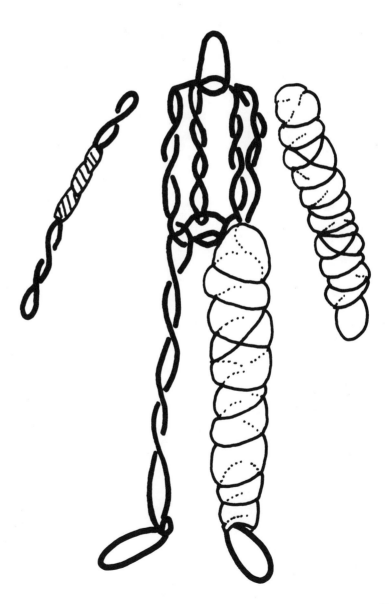

Fig 76 Joe showing construction of the wire frame for the body; the arms are made separately. The cut ends of the wire are bound with tape and then the form of the body is achieved by binding stuffing to the frame

Some more ideas for novelty dolls

1.   Make Louisa with Suffolk puff legs of white cotton. These would then be pantaloons and legs combined.

2.   Louisa can also be made as a turnover doll. Draw a line across the pattern where the waist would be, then place this line to a fold when cutting out the cloth and replace the short dowel with a longer one that extends between the two necks. Use the optional arm pattern and attach in the same way as the arms for Miss Victoria. Dress her as Cinderella in patchwork rags one end and ready for the Ball on the other end. Make a circular skirt rather than a gathered one as it will fall more easily.

3.   Other ideas for turnover dolls might be Mustard Seed, Cobweb, Moth and Pease Blossom from A Midsummer Night's Dream.

4.   Make a felt face mask for Louisa, use the optional arm pattern and dress her in a pyjama lounge suit.

5.   Sew a continuous tube with feet on either end. Simple hands can be formed by tying a knot in the centre of the tube. Figure 77 shows what can be done with this novel body.

Fig 77   Jumping for joy

130

Further reading

There are many books on doll-making and the history of dolls and undoubtedly some will be available in your local library. However, if you have any difficulties the following selection will be useful.

Bachmann, M. and Hausmann, C. *Dolls the Wide World Over* (Harrap, 1973)
Boehn, Max von *Dolls and Puppets* (Cooper Square, New York, 1966)
Coleman, D.S., E.A., and E.J. *The Collector's Encyclopaedia of Dolls* (Robert Hale, 1970)
Coleman, D.S., E.A., and E.J. *The Collector's Book of Dolls' Clothes* (Robert Hale, 1976)
Eaton, F. *Dolls in Colour* (Blandford Press, 1975)
Fettig, H. *Glove and Rod Puppets* (Harrap, 1973)
Gray, I. *Making Dolls* (Studio Vista, 1972)
Greenhowe, J. *Dolls in National and Folk Costume* (Batsford, 1978)
Hillier, M. *Dolls and Dollmakers* (Weidenfeld and Nicolson, 1968)
Hutchings, M. *Dolls and How to Make Them* (Mills and Boon, 1963)
Johnson, Audrey *Dressing Dolls* (Bell, 1969)
King, C.E. *Dolls and Dolls' Houses* (Hamlyn, 1977)
Laury, Jean Ray *Doll Making A Creative Approach* (Van Nostrand Reinhold, 1970)
White, G. *European and American Dolls* (Batsford, 1966)
Witzig, H. and Kuhn, G. *Making Dolls* (Sterling Publishing Co, New York, 1969)
Worrell, E.A. *The Doll Book* (Van Nostrand Reinhold, 1966)

Index

Page numbers in **bold** type denote colour illustrations; page numbers in *italics* denote Figures.